ALEX HOLDER talks about money. Her viral 'Make Them Pay' campaign sought to end the pay gap between men and women; it received backing from the then prime minister, and led to gender pay-gap reporting legislation, which saw the creation of the 2018 mandatory pay-gap audit. She's lived on £15k and £130k, had her gas meter turned off and been named by the *Evening Standard* as a Top 5 Inspiring Female Leader. She is also one of Business Insider's 30 Most Creative Women globally, and writes regularly for *ELLE*, *Grazia*, *Refinery29* and the *Guardian* among others.

OPEN UP

Why Talking About Money Will Change Your Life

ALEX HOLDER

This paperback edition published in 2020

First published in Great Britain in 2019 by
Serpent's Tail,
an imprint of Profile Books Ltd
29 Cloth Fair
London
EC1A 7JQ
www.serpentstail.com

1 3 5 7 9 10 8 6 4 2

Printed and bound in Great Britain by
CPI Group (UK) Ltd, Croydon, CR0 4YY

A CIP catalogue record for this book is available from the British Library.

ISBN 978 1 78816 188 6
eISBN 978 1 78283 516 5

For Mark, who showed me another way to live.

Contents

A note from the author

Apart from named professionals and quoted experts, I've changed the names and sometimes identifying features of people in this book. It turned out, at the time of writing, that to get people talking about money I had to offer them anonymity. Here's hoping that when they've read this book they'll feel differently, and so will you.

WE NEED TO TALK

This is a book about our emotional relationship with money. It's full of conversations about money in everyday life, how we earn it, how we spend it and how it affects our relationships, friendships and career choices. It's for people who want to read a book about life, love, passion, awkward bosses and judgy friends; it's probably not for people who want to read a book about the mathematical intricacies of finance. It might make you feel awkward, but it will never make you feel bored.

1

Look where not talking about money has got us

When I was terrible with money I talked about it. I complained about how far away payday was. I took pride in my reckless spending. I showed off to friends by withdrawing my last £20 from a cashpoint, then running into Tesco to buy two bottles of prosecco on my card before the bank realised I'd taken all my money out. I was proud of how useless I was. Despite buying into the idea that the more money someone has, the better their life is, I felt strangely comfortable being bad with it. 'Reckless 20-something' was a relatively uncomplicated character to play – I was that person, the one who could get their ass in gear to book a flight to Berlin but who never opened a bill. Maybe, because I knew I wasn't earning the most money, I took refuge in bowing out of the competition and just being bad with money. There seemed less shame in staying broke than admitting money mattered.

There was a time when all my friends were open about money. When we were leaving university and trying to get our first jobs, we were all at the bottom of an imagined ladder and there was a pack mentality: us against the world. Sharing benefitted us all. In a couple of conversations we'd know what to expect salary-wise by industry and entry-level position, which for a graduate was pretty invaluable information. Then as we slowly peeled away from each other and into different industries, some of us earning more, some earning less, money became a shameful subject. Perhaps it's because people can literally be placed in a pecking order of highest earner to lowest that we stopped sharing what we earned. No one wanted to feel that they were in a league table with their friends and subject themselves to that kind of direct comparison, so money became a subject to skirt around. The more complicated our lives got, the more it solidified into a taboo subject. As we moved forward as adults, we faced decisions about money on our own: how much salary to ask for, what was a normal amount to pay in rent and whether we could really afford to go to that hen do in Barcelona.

The idea that our salary and the money in our bank account defines us – that it represents our happiness, our power, our status, our popularity, our intelligence and our freedom – is a hugely popular idea that we are constantly encouraged to believe. It's why we protect our salaries to such an extent; we're warned that revealing our number might feel akin to public masturbation or broadcasting a therapy session, that if you spoke about your salary, people would know you too intimately. It was something I completely bought into as a young adult, yet as I've got older I've realised that salary isn't as defining as I first thought. That number doesn't indicate everything; it's not your happiness or your popularity or any of those other identifiers. In fact, I've seen people who earn less be happier than people who earn more. I've learned to see that there are many currencies in life other than money: love, health, time, passion, purpose and freedom. Now I can't help but see how often we sacrifice the other currencies in pursuit of the only one we recognise to the decimal point – money.

The social code dictating that we shouldn't talk about money was invented and perpetuated by the richest of society and trickled down to the rest of us; not talking about money is a privilege of the wealthy. For those who inherit wealth, discussions about money serve no purpose: their funds are secure, they don't need to talk about it. In contrast, if you're not rich then discussing money becomes critical to your survival: 'Where are the cheapest places to buy food?' 'Where are the affordable places to live?' Equally, if you're trying to make it in a new country, or a new city far away from your home town – in New York, or London, or Paris – you are going to want to discuss how the hell people afford rent. If you're a woman and suspect you're being paid less than your male colleagues, the only way you're going to find out is by asking. If you're a person of colour and think you're being charged more for your insurance, you're going to want to make it known. If you can't afford to eat at that restaurant you are going to have to tell your friends.

We've basically allowed privileged people to determine how we talk about money. And as a result, we're stuck in a place where talking about what we earn, spend and save is just too awkward. There is seemingly too much at stake to talk about money with any level of earnestness; everyone is too scared of embarrassing anyone else and too scared of feeling any shame themselves. Also, we don't know how to talk about it. We haven't developed the vocabulary. How do you tell your mum you've got into more debt than you can handle? Why does sharing a money trouble sometimes feel like a request for funds when what you really need is an ear and some advice? Shame feels so intrinsically tied to money. But shame is an emotion we harbour in secret, and so it's possible that if we were more open about money it wouldn't be allowed to fester to such a degree.

I was a sell-out. For years I worked in advertising, selling beer, junk food and clothes on credit to people who couldn't afford them. My job lacked purpose. It left me with little time to myself, and I often went years not exercising, but it did pay me a decent salary. Weirdly I feel more shame admitting I had money than I ever did about not having it. Talking about money when you have it feels crass and materialistic, like you're 'showing off', or suggesting that you're better than someone else – two things my Northern upbringing taught me to scorn. I still feel uncomfortable admitting I'm not in my overdraft, and I sometimes miss the student camaraderie of all being in the same skint boat, even though I appreciate I'm lucky.

I can think of so many conversations with friends lately that have felt inauthentic because money-related parts of the story were missing. Just because I'm no longer a skint student doesn't mean I don't have money issues I need to work through. We all do. When I quit my full-time job to go freelance I didn't really talk to friends about it, because to elicit any real advice I'd have had to talk actual figures. I'm tired of skirting around the subject of money with people I love and trust. It feels ridiculous that I've accompanied a friend to a sexual health clinic but I have no idea how she bought a flat in London.

It's not just our friends' finances we're curious about – every year the BBC has to publish a list of its top earners, and there's not a year it hasn't made front-page news. When *Forbes* reported Kylie Jenner was on track to become the world's first 'self-made billionaire', the Internet wasn't shy in its outrage. 'Self-made' isn't a term that seems to fit someone born into a celebrity family, with huge amounts of wealth and countless assets at their disposal, and the commentators were quick to point this out. When *Grazia* printed a piece by a woman who admitted that despite earning nearly £40k a year, she'd moved back in with her mum and dad and still required handouts from them most months, it incited judgement and online berating, with a minor smattering of empathy and understanding. The attention these 'news' stories attracted proved how starved we are of conversations about individuals and their financial situations; they also proved how much judgement abounds when it comes to talking about money.

Other people's wages are interesting not just because we're nosey but because the more we know about what other people earn, the more we know about our own salary – you can't tell if you're being under- or overpaid without the context of what other people in your industry earn. I would never have known it was time to ask for a pay rise before the day some of my colleagues' wages accidently went public. Someone from accounts had left a notepad lying open in the meeting room of the advertising agency I worked at, and there, written in blue biro, were the names of eight of my colleagues, alongside their current wages and salary increases. That scrawled page of notes was photographed and passed around the agency from person to person to person, and we gorged on those pen marks, each colleague gifting them to another. The wages ranged from £22k to £130k. There was no formal pay structure; instead people earned what they were brave enough to negotiate, which meant the figures were varied and fascinating. The highest earner was (of course) a man. He had a couple more years' experience than me, and was earning £38k more. Based only on the information on that bit of paper I asked for a pay rise and I got it (see, knowledge really is power).

Secrecy keeps pay gaps intact. It puts power in the hands of the employer and it breeds feelings of shame. Transparency has been touted as the answer to addressing pay inequality across gender, age and race, and as the first step to closing the growing income gap between the richest and poorest. It was the 2018 gender pay gap audit that kickstarted a very public conversation about what we earn. Journalists, economists and even Hollywood actors couldn't help but discuss, share and debate other people's wages. Public conversation, the kind that makes newspaper headlines, is needed – it changes society and challenges perceptions. But while we're getting more comfortable with the subject of salaries and remuneration, we still find it difficult to talk about our own money. But the power of transparency can work at an individual level too. One-on-one chats with friends or family is how we first deal with most of life's issues. Talking is healthy and liberating. It's how we share stories and educate each other.

Recently the power of conversation has lifted the stigma from another taboo subject: mental health. We've seen something of a 'coming out', where people are sharing their mental health stories; people seemed to realise that talking and sharing helps. There is now less shame attached to having anxiety or suffering from panic-attacks. Ten years ago it wasn't something you spoke about; now people even put 'I'm having a mental health day' in their out-of-office email.

When a celebrity shares her experiences of postnatal depression it makes thousands of women feel normal. Sharing liberates the individual and helps others feel less alone. We need a movement like this for money and personal finances, and I'm hoping that the public pay gap conversations prompt personal ones. I'm not saying you should reveal your salary to the person sat next to you on the bus, but I am looking for some affinity between how we discuss sex or mental health and how we discuss money – whether in the public sphere, online, in the press and at policy level. And on an individual level, we should feel we can chat about money with people we trust, in spaces we feel safe.

We go through life rarely discussing money, which means that a lot of what we learn from our parents and the world we grew up in remains unchallenged. Without realising it, how we think, behave and relate to money often doesn't have anything to do with what we earn and our present situation, but instead can be traced back to a few formative experiences. If money was tight when you were growing up, or you have memories of a parent being made redundant, you might find spending feels painful. If your parents were very strict with you and enforced saving, spending recklessly could be your way of rebelling. If you were surrounded by messages that having money is greedy and corrupts you, then you're probably not going to become rich. We're never going to break these habits or create new beliefs if we don't learn how other people think about money … or indeed spend it. To understand our own relationship with money we need to hear different stories from other people.

As well as having little knowledge of how the people around us spend or save, it's also been made really easy for us to distance ourselves from the numbers of our own everyday spending: we have Apple Pay, we have one-click checkouts, and Amazon's Alexa means passing thoughts can become purchases in seconds. Then at the other end of the spectrum, mortgage products and loans can be so baffling in their complexity that they create a different kind of avoidance: 'I don't understand it, so I'm not even going to try.' We have to process a lot as an individual, with little by way of straightforward help, and are expected to come out on top. No wonder we've created a whole load of avoidance tactics.

I often wonder was I so bad with money for so long because I only heard money stories from friends who were bad with money? It definitely wasn't the case that all my friends were living on takeaways and had their electricity cut off (as I was), it's just that those were the only sort of stories I heard. No one told me about their savings accounts and pay negotiations. I guess those stories fell into the gauche conversation pile, which is such a shame, as they're the ones I could have learned from. Just as I'm sure some friends learned what not to do from my tales of being bad with money, I could have learned from them about pension schemes and compound interest.

Here's the thing – we don't know how society might function if we spoke about money. But we do know that the wealth gap between the richest and the poorest is increasing. We know women and people of colour are routinely paid less than white men. We know that millennials are struggling to buy property. Talking won't fix those things immediately – but it could be an important start.

Americans are a little further ahead of us Brits in tackling the taboo around money. Gaby Dunn has spearheaded many awkward conversations in her brilliant podcast *Bad with Money*. She's revealed the actual numbers of her bank account, challenged the American dream of economic mobility and spoken about what it's like to have people recognise you from YouTube fame while serving tables for minimum wage. Refinery29 is the leading global media company focused on young women, and their most popular content – *Money Diaries* – began on their American site. On the surface *Money Diaries* simply features women tracking their spending, but in reality it is addictive reading, because it reveals a truth about millennial lives that was hidden before. But here in the UK we're still behind on the conversation, especially the personal, which creates a strange imbalance in our knowledge – before I wrote this book, I didn't know my sister's salary, but I did know the amount of child maintenance One Direction's Louis Tomlinson has to pay.

Awkwardness stands in the way of knowledge and possible liberation. If we're afraid to broach the subject of personal wealth, how can we challenge its inequalities? It's not easy for everybody to talk about money: some people are just too vulnerable, whether in a zero-hours contract or living in a precarious rental. At the other end, some risk their privilege, like a man sharing his salary with female colleagues. It's important to question why we're uncomfortable, and what we have to offer (not just what we have to lose) by talking. Because sharing information and stories might just be the first step to a more even sharing of resources.

I recently spoke on a panel for a big brand. They offered to pay me £150, which I didn't think to negotiate. Another freelancer kindly let me know that she'd negotiated £250, and she explained why she was telling me: 'It doesn't benefit me if you're accepting less money, it means they'll keep offering £150 and it drives the market rate down.' It's true, I should have followed my instinct that £150 felt low, especially as the brand we were working for evidently had money. And yes, there was definitely some awkwardness when the other freelancer told me she was paid more, but the benefit to both of us completely outweighed that momentary weirdness of discussing our pay, and next time I'll be sure to negotiate my rate.

Let's learn from what we've seen happen when people started to share their experiences of mental health issues. There is far less judgement than people anticipated, and so much more empathy. In *Daring Greatly*, Brené Brown talks about the power of leaning into vulnerability. 'What most of us fail to understand ... is that vulnerability is also the cradle of the emotions and experiences that we crave,' says Dr Brown. 'Vulnerability is the birthplace of love, belonging, joy, courage, empathy and creativity.' It feels time to allow ourselves to feel vulnerable (even to the shame of having more money than someone else).

Which brings us to – why this book? Well, frankly there aren't enough conversations happening in real life, so we're starting them here for you. I know that talking about money is hard, but this book will show you that you are not alone. I'm hoping it will make you feel understood, and won't make you cringe too much. We all have our own money stories. I have lived many: I've lived on £15k in London and on the other end at £130k. I have been a wage slave and I've put myself through the freelance hustle. I've been happy and I've been sad, and these emotional states have not always correlated with my bank balance. I'm white, I'm a cis-female, I identified as Northern working class and now as some kind of media-London middle class. But this isn't just my story, it's a collection, a rally, a coming together of many stories and viewpoints and thoughts. It's not about one person having the answer; it's about finding your answer. Currently we're as confused as a society as we are as individuals. I'm tired of navigating a culture that values possessions and money but vilifies the rich, one that flits between painting the poor as virtuous before demonising them. I'm exhausted by how we obsess over who has what but discourage any conversation, or even verbal acknowledgement of our own finances.

This book is packed with real-life case studies, dilemmas, awkward social situations and expert advice. Here we learn from others, from their experiences and their actual bank statements. We learn from people who are good with money, people who aren't and people who are in a really complicated relationship with … money. Ultimately we'll learn that it's not about how much or how little you have, it's how your money works for you, it's how you feel about it. If money is a universal, common currency, then you'd think its meaning in our lives would come down to maths, but it doesn't: it's emotional. I believe we can change our relationship with money through the power of conversation, and while talking isn't the complete journey, it's part of the path. Here, we look at how to discuss student debt, gender pay gaps, millennial financial resentment, the problem with the title 'self-made' and the minimum wage. We question how class, race and privilege affect the money we have and therefore the lives we live.

This book dismantles some of the cultural taboos surrounding money, especially those that can affect relationships with people we love. We're going to look at what it's like to earn more (or less) than your friends, how to be financially intimate with your partner, how to examine your money anxieties, why you should stare debt in the face, what it means to go freelance or take a full-time job, how to ask for more money and how to live on less. We're going to celebrate how it feels to spend the money you have on things you love. We're going to explain why you feel the way you do about shopping and why rich people are vilified. We get to the bottom of why hen and stag dos cost so much. We're going to look at the relationship between money and mental health. And we're going to arm you with an answer to the tired question: should we just split the bill down the middle?

2

I want to talk about my advance for this book

A couple of years ago I was asked to talk at an event for women in the music industry. It was at Google HQ in London, the topic was equal pay and we were covering the usual angles: asking for what you are worth and the importance of transparency in closing the pay gap.

'We should start the talk by revealing our salaries,' I said to my co-host.

'Yes! We can project them above our heads!' she replied.

We never did reveal our salaries. Feeling like the hypocrites we evidently were, my co-host and I stood in front of a room of successful women and talked brazenly about why they should ask their male colleagues what they earned and challenge their managers for greater transparency. The talk was a rallying cry for more openness and bravery when it came to talking about money at work. Our slides were punchy, our words and facts seemed convincing. Just not convincing enough to get us to reveal our own salaries. That would have been far too awkward. Weird even. It was 2016, and although lots of people were starting to debate the taboo around salaries, it was still a step too far to actually say your salary out loud to a room full of strangers.

In all the chatter and planning for that talk, my co-host and I didn't even end up telling each other our respective salaries. I remember feeling in my gut the absolute need for transparency, but couldn't reconcile this with the nakedness I would have felt if I had revealed my number. Our relationship with money really is messy: it's not an honest one. I wanted to feel one way about it, but couldn't. My emotions fought any logic my brain tried to provide. After all, I had grown up hearing that talking about money could only ever be a bad, shameful thing to do.

What was I scared of exactly? That the women in the audience might have hurled their plastic cups of white wine at me? That people would still be whispering my salary two weeks later? That they'd presume I didn't understand their lives because what I earned was so different to them? Money can be so divisive, and I was scared people would reject me based on what I earned.

But I've since started to practise what I preach and the worst hasn't happened. So right here, I want to talk about the advance for this book. It's a conversation that, initially, I often left hanging. I'd tell people excitedly that I had a book deal, and they'd inevitably ask 'did you get an advance?' After a quick 'yeah!' the conversation would stop. Abruptly.

This is a book about our emotional relationship with money and why we need to talk about it. That I might feel I can't talk about its advance – well, I can see the irony. I worried about telling people the amount for so many reasons; I worried it would compromise my publisher and my agent and ultimately that by exposing myself I would be exposing others too. I mainly worried that it would compromise the book, this book. That you would think, 'Oh, that's not a large amount, it can't be very good' or 'That's too much!'

At the same time I feel immensely proud and privileged that I have been given an advance to write a book.

The advance was £12,500.

There. That wasn't nearly as hard as I imagined it would be. My literary agency takes 15 per cent. I receive half up front, the book has taken four solid months of writing and out of that money I've had to pay some of the people interviewed for their time and have employed transcribers.

I will never know if it devalued the book in your mind. That might be a lot of money to you – or it might seem like pocket money. Either way, I hope that sharing that figure might help someone, maybe even you, work something out about your life. Maybe you've thought about writing but haven't known how or if it pays. The only book deals we hear about are the six-figure ones but even they can be deceptive; a headline-grabbing '£100k four-book deal' is only £25k a book, and if a book takes a year to write that deal means that the author will be on a very average salary. Apart from those large deals reported in the press, I don't know the actual amount of any other author's advance.

I realise revealing my advance isn't the same as admitting I'm drowning in debt, but maybe by bringing all money to the surface we'll remove it of its power to shame. This isn't about only encouraging people who have money to talk about it, it's about integrating money conversations into our daily lives. If we stop diverting the conversation the moment it gets to our personal finances, then maybe when there comes a time that you need to stand up for yourself, or ask an 'impertinent' question, or just be honest with friends, you'll feel you can. And I can now say what I couldn't at Google HQ ... practising transparency is really not that scary a thing to do.

3

How people feel about the money they earn

SPOILER! The rich don't feel rich.

I began by asking a range of people (of different ages, genders, sexualities, ethnicities and classes, at various life stages) two simple questions: 'How much do you earn?' and 'How do you feel about it?' It quickly became apparent that no one feels great about the money they earn. Whether someone earned minimum wage or £200k a year, nearly everyone was dissatisfied. The answers became homogenised: 'not enough' was the general sentiment. So I began to also ask, 'What does rich mean to you?' I asked a 30-year-old woman earning £8 per hour as a market researcher and she gave a simple answer, 'Anyone on £12 per hour.' Another woman earning £8 per hour paused, thought about it for a moment and then came back with '£20 an hour'. A single mum I asked didn't respond with an hourly rate. Instead she said, 'Anyone who doesn't have to worry about money.'

It's all relative. When the *Wall Street Journal* set out to find the definition of rich they discovered that people generally defined rich as double what they currently have, so a venture capitalist worth £3m would class someone with £6m as rich. And someone on £50k a year would consider a peer earning a six-figure salary rich.

You know what I hardly ever hear when I ask people to define rich? 'Me.' Only one person I spoke to, a woman who earns a salary of £75k per year from her own business, came close to defining herself as rich, but she still couldn't quite say it: 'I think I am very comfortable with my earnings. I don't feel like I am poor at all. I don't feel that I am rich, but I feel blessed.' I saw rejection of the title 'rich' again and again. 'Rich' is always someone else, both because of its negative baggage – who wants to admit they're greedy or smug? – but also it seems we live in an age of dissatisfaction, reducing the world to a series of things we don't have.

Research shows that any amount we earn over £50k doesn't make us any happier. Yet we're also sold the idea of an upwards trajectory, that we'll continue to get pay rises as our seniority increases, that our children will have better – and for 'better' read 'wealthier' – lives than us, that there is a 'property ladder' to climb, that a more comfortable life exists somewhere in the future. I've had to recalibrate my own brain lately to the fact that my life, by monetary standards, isn't going to get progressively richer. I won't be driving a better car next year than I am now. I'll still be driving my fifteen-year-old Volvo, it'll just be a sixteen-year-old Volvo. Did I warn you that this book isn't about getting rich? I hope so. I'll tell you why it's not about getting rich: because having more money just means wanting more money. If more money is your goal you will literally never get there, because there is always more to get. Our expectations increase and increase.

As one very rich (by my standards at least – he earns around £260k per year) entrepreneur who lives in Norfolk told me: 'I think "rich" is always one rung further up the ladder than you currently are. I used to think rich people got taxis. Then I got to that stage. Then I thought rich people were able to buy a suit on a whim. Then I got to that stage. Then I thought rich people went on nice holidays with other rich people. Then I got to that stage. Then I thought rich people had nice houses and cars, etc. Then I got to that stage. Then I thought rich people flew business and had second homes and stuff. Then I got to that stage. Now I look at houses that cost £3m and think, "Who the fuck are these *rich* people?" Maybe I'll get there one day and then I'll look at houses that cost £10m and think they're rich people. It never ends, and all the while I'm still spending every penny I have each month and never thinking of myself as rich.'

In other words, being rich doesn't always mean you feel it. I heard this same sentiment echoed by a London-based tech CEO: 'By the vast majority of standards, I'm very rich (and very lucky to be so). But I don't think of myself as rich, day to day. That's partly because of the relativity. Despite earning far more than I did when I was younger, and growing up in a family that had to make the most of what we had, I don't feel like I lead a more "rich" lifestyle than I ever have. It clearly is a far more expensive lifestyle, but it doesn't feel it. I always think of "rich" as a more lavish life than mine, relatively. Or at least having the money to make that life possible. Despite earning £200k a year, I somehow have no money left at the end of the month, with nothing to show for it except paying off a mortgage, supporting two kids and going on a nice holiday each year.'

So if the country's top earners still don't feel rich, how are the rest of us, the majority, supposed to feel about our money? I remember getting my first notable pay rise, from £15k to £20k. That pay rise marked the moment I didn't have to choose between the bus or a Tesco sandwich. It meant I stopped stealing dishwasher tablets from work, and finally I could offer to buy a round in the pub. I remember the first time that hiked-up pay cheque hit my bank account. I remember seeing the numbers and feeling so rich. The next month it still felt good, but didn't quite match the elation of the first month, and then it became normal, and after normal came the feeling of not enough. And from talking to people who earn way above the national average (which is currently £27,195) I realise they feel the same as I did on £20k – the general sentiment of our conversations was, 'I have everything I need, but it still doesn't seem like enough.'

This isn't really about rich people not feeling rich. All of the top earners I spoke to understand that they earn a lot. It's just that their expectations of life have exceeded their means, or they know, and compare themselves unfavourably to, people who earn more. Many of us, no matter where we stand on the spectrum, do the same – we look up, compare and want more. I started with how rich people feel about money so we can quash early on the idea that more money would solve everything. Of course, it solves some things, like paying rent or eating, but it's important to remember that happiness is not one of them. One of our main refrains, whether we earn a lot or very little, is 'If I was rich then …' Only by talking to those with the most and asking them how they feel about the money they have do we find out that money isn't necessarily making them happier. In order to know how people feel about money we need to talk about it – because conversations stop us from making presumptions or chasing fantasies that don't exist.

Which brings us to the question of – what is enough? 'Enough' is as hard to quantify as 'rich'. For one thing, it can be just as subjective. How do you judge what is enough to live on or to be comfortable, when even the world's top earners think that what they have is not enough? 'A lot of the issues we have surrounding money can't be solved with more money,' Simonne Gnessen, a financial therapist, tells me. 'How we feel about money is far more important than how much we earn.' If we don't feel we have enough, then earning more isn't necessarily the solution. A better tactic might be changing whom we compare ourselves with. How we feel about money is often relative to how we compare to those directly around us. Privilege is relative. If you're reading this book having come across it in England chances are you're in the world's top 2 per cent of richest people. Yet knowing you are richer than a factory worker in Ethiopia (earning an average of 15p per hour) isn't very comforting if you can't afford to buy your kids the things they say they need.

'Enough' is complex. It's entangled with emotion. If you've spent your wages on knee-high boots and therefore can't afford lunch, are you allowed to say you're broke? When people say they have 'money worries' they might mean the strife that comes with paying off a mortgage, or trying to make rent, or keeping up a lifestyle which includes their kids going to a 'good school'. We've seen the generational outrage when millennials moan about the housing crisis while eating an avocado brunch.

But although 'enough' can sometimes feel hopelessly

subjective, it is also an important metric – after all, there is such a thing as not enough to survive. Since 1998 the UK government has enforced minimum wage legislation, which for an adult over 25 is currently £7.83 per hour. This means that someone in full-time employment working 37.5 hours a week will take home £1,146.96 per month after tax and other deductibles. But there is a strong argument that the minimum wage is not enough to live on. The Living Wage Foundation is a campaigning organisation whose work includes calculating how much someone needs for the minimum standard of living. Right now it's calculated above the minimum wage at £8.75 per hour across the UK and £10.20 per hour in London. Although it has no legal status, it has had a large influence in the past years, and many employers, including IKEA, Burberry and Aviva, now pay it.

I spoke to Donald Hirsch, who leads the research for the Living Wage Foundation, and who unpacked what is meant by a 'living wage': 'Our definition of what we mean by a minimum standard of living obviously includes food, clothes and shelter, but it's more than that. It's about having the choices and opportunity that you need to participate in society.' They come to their figure by consulting the public, using focus groups whose members have been selected jury style – so there is a mixture of earnings and different social backgrounds. They ask the groups what they think constitutes a 'decent life' based on 'needs not wants'. Donald tells me how everyone in the focus groups, whether they themselves are rich or poor, generally agree on what is a 'minimum stand of living'. From these focus groups a list is drawn up of everything that the group believes you need to live – from rent, bread and milk to a smartphone, a travel pass, hair straighteners and the occasional babysitter – and the Living Wage is calculated from this list.

I ask Donald about the inclusion on the list of personal grooming and tech items, and whether any are divisive. 'There are things that would have seemed like luxuries in the past, which are really quite necessary now in order to participate in society. There may have been a time and a place where if children went to school in torn clothes that would have been acceptable because that's what all the other kids were doing, but that's not the case now,' he replies. 'A mobile phone might not have been a necessity twenty or thirty years ago, but it is a necessity now because you need it [in order] to function. Just as there is a standard for personal grooming, which is why a product like hair straighteners are included for women.' And alcohol? 'People accept that alcohol in moderation and in a social setting is very much part of our society. If you couldn't afford to ever go out with a mate to have a drink that would mean you are not really living at the sort of minimum level we are talking about.' Defining what is enough is always going to be relative. What the UK classes as enough is different to what another country might define it as, and what is enough today might not be enough in the future.

So how does someone earning a 'living wage' feel about their salary? 'They call my job a "hygienist", which is basically posh for cleaner.' Darren is so open with me about how he earns and spends money. He takes home £1,470 as a full-time night cleaner for a warehouse in Doncaster, and tops it up by collecting fridge-freezers going free on Gumtree and then selling them. In fact, it's on Gumtree where I meet Darren.

He's 30, doesn't have any kids and lives alone in a bedsit

attic conversion, where the rent is £90 a week, 'which I always pay first, so I know I don't have to worry about it,' he tells me. 'I am bad with money; I get payday loans. The majority of the time it's to pay some debt off.' Three years ago Darren took out a £6k loan with Lloyds. 'The bank kept getting in touch, "You can get a loan, you can get a loan." So I took one out, then I got my overdraft extended by a couple of grand and now I use Wonga. I mean it's normal, isn't it? It's a part of life; these loan shops are all over the place, aren't they?' Darren is stuck in a cycle of debt. Every month he takes out payday loans, which then come out of next month's salary, and then he repeats the cycle the next month: 'When your bank account is really low, you feel depressed. If I don't have money I feel depressed, as bad as it sounds, but I feel that way. I like to go to the seaside, buy some clothes, do some food shopping, like it's normal. It's nowt different to what anyone else is doing. Well, I guess, maybe if you're on benefits you can't do it.'

I ask Darren how much money he needs to not feel depressed. He says a hundred pounds makes him feel safe: 'I need to have a certain amount in there, a buffer like. If not I can feel it in myself. I start to think about what might happen. Something might go on my car. Someone might want to do something. I like to think I can be spontaneous.' In other words, having a safety net. Darren's experience connects to what the Living Wage Foundation is trying to assess and to make sure a Living Wage covers those elements of life that make it worth living.

Syeda is 23 and works in the Peckham branch of McDonald's. She says her wage, which is 62p above the minimum McDonald's are required to pay her, is 'slave driving' and 'criminal'. 'I work for £8 an hour. If you work the night shift you only get £9 an hour, £1 extra for when you're meant to be in bed! Man, that doesn't feel right.' I ask her if she discusses her outrage with colleagues. 'We don't get to talk; every minute of every hour is filled with tasks to do. There is no chatting.' Although Syeda was angry about the amount she is paid, she wasn't as disparaging about the life she leads. She works part-time earning about £450 a month, and lives at home with her parents. She pays her mum and dad £200 a month for rent and food, saves £50 and spends the rest on National Lottery tickets and drinks with friends.

Elaine also lives with her mum and dad. 'I feel so guilty doing what I do because really I'm supported by my parents.' Elaine is a stand-up comedian and an auditioning actor, but neither of these earns her money, and so she 'pulls pints' part-time. Elaine's job pays her minimum wage plus tips, and while this isn't enough to live on, she's lucky enough to live with her parents. But she feels duplicitous about this privilege: 'I feel that if I make it as a stand-up, I can't be as proud as someone who might have supported themselves. I know it's not the Pity Olympics, but in the stand-up world there's an attitude that it's brave to be broke. And yet I don't feel broke; I still get to go home to a house with the central heating on full blast.'

Elaine hasn't spoken to her friends in the comedy scene about her feelings. Instead she harbours guilt alone. But rather than feeling guilty, she should feel lucky – and recognise that luck. Ignoring privilege isn't going to diversify the comedy scene. It's possible that a lot of Elaine's comedy peers are in similar situations – being helped out by other people or just scraping by. Perhaps if they shared and compared more they might be able to collectively address the economic issues of breaking into comedy rather than Elaine feeling impotent guilt alone. Elaine wasn't the only person I spoke to who added a verbal privilege disclaimer when talking about career choice. I notice both in my own personal conversations with colleagues and friends and when listening to podcast hosts, panel speakers or wider media, how often people caveat any success with 'obviously with parents who live in London/ being cis/being white/being Oxford-educated I recognise my own privilege.' It's interesting that these elements of people's lives and upbringing have become something to apologise for rather than simply acknowledge. There's a balance to be found, that doesn't ignore privilege, but is also not self-flagellating. It's about being honest about the luck involved in our successes, whilst not minimising any effort and achievement.

I ask Syeda about her friends and how she feels in comparison to them. She tells me her richest friend earns £13 an hour as a plumber. I ask what her richest friend gets to do that she can't – how does that extra £5 per hour separate her life from theirs? 'They drive.' When I asked people what they couldn't afford that they felt should be within their means, cars came up a lot. Darren was left £20k when he was 19 and 'blew it' in five months, but at least he learned to drive during that time. The DSA estimates that the average cost of lessons for a learner driver to pass a test is £1,128, which is nearly to the pound what someone working full-time on minimum wage will take home in a month. That's before the cost of a test and a car and the insurance and the road tax and MOT and petrol and servicing. Driving becomes emotive because it is one of those conveniences people expect in their life, when in most cases driving requires a huge amount of both time and money, which may be beyond many people's means.

'Being rich means being able to put your car in for an MOT and service without stressing out. It is loving the house you live in and being able to get a plumber in on the weekend when your wall-hung toilet falls off the wall. Being able to have the odd date night and afford the babysitter.' Bella is 39, has two children, and she and her husband have a combined income of £78k. They go on a two-week European beach holiday every year and live in a three-bedroom house with a garden, and I love that she defines rich as basically keeping her car running and stopping her house from crumbling around her. And that's what you can't do if you're at the lower end of earning. A car is a liability – actually all possessions are liabilities. If you have £30 of disposable income per week, are you going to spend some of it on a new knob for a kitchen cabinet? Or some WD-40? Probably not.

People often cite 'not having to think about money' as the benefit of having more money. The tech CEO on £200k who said he didn't live a rich lifestyle also added: 'I don't really have to *think* about money. We take the kids out to pizza places regularly, without thinking about it. Or meet friends for drinks, without thinking about it. If I lose some headphones, I buy a new pair without really worrying about it. So one definition of rich might be about being able to do simple things without ever thinking about them. In that sense I'm rich.'

For a very different reason, Mason, a 28-year-old from Skegness, talks about the relief of not having to think about money. He spent seven months in jail for 'silly behaviour', and now works full-time as a warehouse picker and packer. He recognises the mental toll that worrying about money can have: 'At least you don't have to pay rent in prison. You get your three meals a day, get your PlayStation and have a smoke-up with your friends. It's like being at home really. You're looked after. A lot of people that I know have been to prison and they like it. You don't have money troubles in prison and that's a relief.'

It says something about the power that money has to stress us out, when prison is described as a relief.

Susie, a PhD student in Liverpool, makes a £13k salary work for her and her seven-year-old daughter. 'I shop in charity shops, we eat a lot of pasta and we get the bus,' she tells me. She's happy to talk about their frugality: that she makes a small amount go a long way and 'can make a curry for 90p' is a legitimate source of pride in itself. Susie feels virtuous. I can see that she sees it as an achievement, that in a society that is urging us all to spend money all the time, she doesn't. Talking to her I see how much discipline it takes to bring up a kid and remain on budget – it doesn't look easy or fun. I can see why she takes such pride in making it work, but I'm also left thinking about the toll it might take on her mental health in the long run.

So what did I learn from asking people intimate questions about their salaries? Mainly that while very little money can cause stress and misery, at the other end of the scale more money might mean ease of mind, but it doesn't correlate with greater happiness. Research had already told me that, but it wasn't until I talked to people about how they felt about the money they earned that I finally took it in and understood – money can make your life comfortable, yes, but more money just makes you want even more money, and that treadmill doesn't look that appealing. It seems that one of the healthiest things to do is to take a moment and appreciate when we have enough.

Financial therapists – what are they?

This book is full of advice from financial experts. There are the experts you might expect: business psychologists, economists, financial advisors and CEOs of banks, but I've also spoken to a lot of financial therapists, a fairly new breed of professional. It was born in America – of course it was, I can't think of anything more un-British – but the fact that they have started to be adopted over here might be evidence that we are ready to start talking about money.

But what exactly are they? Let me explain. A couple of years ago I met financial therapist Simonne Gnessen (or as she calls herself – a financial coach) for an article I was writing for *ELLE* magazine. The conversation we had was unlike any other conversation I'd had about money. We didn't talk in numbers, percentages and tax brackets; instead we spoke about life choices, anxieties and freedom. Sitting and talking about my money situation was extraordinarily liberating and useful. I realised that chatting openly about my personal finances was something I'd never done before. That single conversation gave me the confidence to try out being a freelance writer and halve my salary in the process. One of my best decisions ever. I wanted to capture some of the understanding I felt when I was with Simonne, so throughout this book I will introduce you to different financial therapists. Some have different specialisms, such as couples counselling, LGBTQI money or career changes, but they are all experts in money and its emotional, behavioural and relational hurdles.

In America to call yourself a financial therapist you have to be accredited by the Financial Therapy Association. The UK doesn't yet have an equivalent accreditation, which is why Brits use the term 'coach'. Some have a background in psychology and others started out as financial advisors. As practitioners they all use talking therapy to improve their clients' relationship with money, like a typical therapy session except one in which the therapist is holding your bank statements.

Although financial therapists are equipped with financial training, the conversations I've had with them are about the 'whys' behind our behaviour around money, not the 'hows'. Turns out, to no one's surprise, that emotions, mental health, hang-ups from childhood and social pressure are a big part of what's to blame for our rocky relationship with money. Financial therapists are not something readily available to everybody (not least because a session with one starts at £250), so I've used them throughout this book by asking for their explanation and advice on a variety of different situations. I'm so grateful to all the therapists I spoke to, and I think you will be too.

4

Money and shame

Why do we need to talk about shame? Because it's the thing that stops us talking about money.

Generally when I tell people I'm writing a book about why we need to talk about money they start chatting at me like they've just come back from a silent retreat; it's as if they are starved for a conversation about money. They start talking and don't stop. Finally they have been given a reason, an excuse to say out loud all the things they have never been allowed to say before. Some start listing details of their outgoings, details so mundane they are fascinating, others immediately go deeper, musing about why their brother's attitude towards money differs so massively from their own.

Then there is an altogether different reaction. One of slight disgust, of judgement, of stand-offishness. Many politely stepped back, avoided further conversation and escaped me at the earliest opportunity. Writing this book was an awkward time; I made quite a divisive dinner party guest. When a friend of a friend asked me what I was up to and I told him, he immediately clenched and asked outright,

'Why do you think it's a good idea, to talk about money? Why would anyone need to do that?'

My answer should have included how poor and vulnerable people are suffering most from the silence, that the wealth gap is increasing, that women are routinely underpaid and that money is the greatest cause of anxiety for Britons. I should have pointed out that we know transparency can help solve these issues, and that conversation is what roots us to other humans. If I'm feeling stressed I call my best friend, if I want advice I talk to a colleague, an evening of conversation in the pub is my happiest place, yet a huge topic that governs a lot of my life – where I work, where I live, what I wear – is verbally out of bounds.

I didn't say any of that; instead I felt his shame, a shame that he didn't want to surface and I didn't want to aggravate. Even in small doses, shame is an emotion so powerful that it stops us thinking logically. We don't want to feel it so we suppress the cause. One of the main reasons money is so linked to shame is because we're not meant to talk about it. As Dr Brené Brown writes, 'Shame derives its power from being unspeakable.' And as she said in her TED Talk, 'Listening to Shame', 'If you put shame in a Petri dish, it needs three things to grow exponentially: secrecy, silence and judgement.' We have trapped ourselves in a cycle – we don't talk about money so it creates shame and the shame stops us talking about it.

In a popular essay entitled 'The Return of Shame', writer Andy Crouch helpfully pulls apart guilt from shame: 'In a guilt culture you know you are good or bad by what your conscience feels. In a shame culture you know you are good or bad by what your community says about you, by whether it honors or excludes you.' I think about the many years I hid all of my sanitary products, tucking a Tampax up my sleeve to take one to the bathroom and being mortified when my new boyfriend saw a box of tampons in my dresser drawer. I know what you're thinking – what does this have to do with our shame surrounding money? Well, recently campaigners have been talking openly about periods. When Kiran Gandhi free-bled as she ran the 2015 London Marathon, she said she did it to help end the stigmatisation of period blood: 'I ran with blood dripping down my legs for sisters who don't have access to tampons. I ran to say, it does exist.' Seeing Kiran run with a stain spreading between her legs was a radical sight, but since then a mainstream advert for Bodyform has featured actual period blood rather than blue water. The shame that surrounded periods has started to dissipate, and this effect has trickled down to me. I no longer stress about hiding my tampons, and importantly I talk far more openly about reproductive health with my girl friends. Only good things have come from us facing what was once deemed a shameful subject. Shelters will now put out a very public request for sanitary products to be donated, and the women who need them feel safer asking for them. We're talking about how to make sure periods don't keep young girls out of school, and openly discussing the symptoms of ovarian cancer.

Shame is a social construct, and things that were once shameful don't need to remain shameful for ever. The conversation surrounding money is at a critical point. Many of us are putting our head above the parapet and asking, 'Wait, why am I not meant to talk about this?' 'Why does it make me feel so uncomfortable?' To get to a place of no shame we are going to have to have some radical conversations, and there are going to have to be radical actions, but not everyone has to free-bleed publicly.

What is so shameful about money? What shame have we allowed to grow behind that giant wall of silence? Well, there's poor shame, but there is also rich shame. I spoke to a woman who had a family business go under and then landed a great job, and she said, 'In eighteen months I went from being the most broke out of my friends to one of the higher earners. What's strange is that I felt the same shame about earning the least as I do about earning the most.' In the absence of real conversation, increasingly all we have are what the media portrays, and those portrayals are often extreme and unfair. The rich are painted as greedy, privileged and un-empathetic; in some papers 'rich' has even become a term of insult. And the poor are depicted as untrustworthy scroungers. In our society we talk derisively about the poor; they're often painted as benefit thieves or money wasters. The media mocks them for their spending decisions. The word 'chav' doesn't just describe someone as poor and lower-class, it also defines them as a lout. By our cultural standards there is no right amount of money to have – even 'the squeezed middle' are derided by the papers on a daily basis.

In his book *Shame: Free Yourself, Find Joy, and Build True Self-Esteem*, Joseph Burgo puts shame into four categories, one of which is 'exclusion and being left out'. Everyone wants to feel like they belong, to feel part of a pack, and yet money has the ability to lift you out of a social group – it can seat you in economy while your friends are flying first, or render you unable to relate to your cousin's struggle. It's why I've felt shame about what I earn no matter what the number was, as it's rarely the same as someone else. I thought that my number always placed me above someone – or below them. But I've learned that if you're talking to people you love and trust, and no one is showing off, knowing what people earn doesn't have to be shameful or awkward. It's actually illuminating: 'Oh, so that's how you afforded a flat in London!' I hear myself exclaiming. Also, it's hard to resent a friend her huge salary and Mercedes when you know she's working all the hours in a misogynistic law firm to afford it. Conversation has made me realise that just because a friend earns more money than me, it doesn't make them immune to money worries – I earn more than I did ten years ago, but money can still be as stressful now. It's hard for shame to find a place in honest conversation, even if the conversation is about typically shameful topics such as earning more or less than someone, losing your job or receiving a large inheritance.

There's another type of shame, which Burgo categorises as 'disappointed expectation', 'when you set out to do something and you fail'. Well, you instantly know why this is connected to money. It's a familiar feeling – everyone else but me seems to know what they're doing. As Thomas Faupl, a San Francisco-based financial therapist explains, 'you can feel intense shame over not being able to provide for yourself or your family in a way that's expected. Many of us weren't taught how to manage money and how to make sure we have enough to cover the basics. Sometimes just keeping on top of finances feels too difficult. It doesn't compute in our brains, and there is shame around that.'

It's painted as a simple subject, yet money is complicated. We don't talk about how we earn or manage our money or share tips or stresses. Instead we put on a brave face, whether we stupidly spent our rent on Jägerbombs last night or not, which leaves us all thinking that everyone else is fine, and cue shame if you're not.

Have you ever noticed that when you feel shame you want to hide? That's kind of its purpose as an emotion, to protect us from danger. It makes us want to hide in a cave or never get out of bed. It makes us want to keep things to ourselves and bury them. Another of Burgo's shame categories is 'unwanted exposure'. Having a naked selfie go viral is unwanted exposure, just as having your salary left on a notepad in a meeting room for all your colleagues to read is unwanted exposure. It's this category where money and shame most intersect. Society's rule that we shouldn't reveal any details of our personal finances means everyone is susceptible to exposure. Because of the scarcity of information, something as boring as your bank statement is a treasure trove. So we hide it, we keep quiet about it and we remain complicit in keeping money a shameful topic.

Talking about something honestly is fundamental to an anti-shame movement. I'm not saying everybody needs to shout about their last pay rise; I realise free-bleeding is for a few radicals. You might not have to do anything other than recognise your discomfort in talking about money. Try to sit with that shame. Don't immediately shut down the conversation when it comes to your money or somebody else's. Acknowledge that money isn't inherently shameful, and that we're still suffering a hang-up from previous generations. Just as we learned to talk about sexuality, we can learn to talk about money.

5

They fuck you up your mum and dad ...

Do you ever consider therapy and then think, 'But I can't be arsed with all that mum and dad stuff.' Yeah, I get you. When I'm feeling stressed I want a quick fix. I want strategies, I don't want to have to think about that time I was eight and my best friend dumped me. But, sometimes, for clarity as an adult we need to look back.

From what I saw, my parents both had brilliant work ethics but a sporadic relationship with saving, spending and credit. I entered adult life with a similar attitude, although I wasn't conscious that I was repeating what I'd grown up with ... until I went to see Simonne Gnessen, a financial therapist. Like all therapists she was curious about my childhood and my relationship with my mum and dad – except unlike other therapists she was also armed with my bank statements. Ten minutes into our session she asked, 'Are you more like your mum or your dad in terms of your spending habits?' You mean my dad who walks for an hour passing three Waitroses to get to a Lidl, or my mum who always finds money for a holiday no matter what? I had expected her first challenge to be around the fact that I regularly do an Amazon splurge at one in the morning, or the miscellaneous cash I withdraw at other ungodly hours. Her question was relevant though. As with much of our adult behaviour, many of our beliefs about money are founded in childhood.

The social class we're born into, how much money our family had growing up, how our parents earned and spent money and who they socialised with all affect how we behave around money as adults. We think we're our own people, but we inherit all sorts of habits and quirks from the few people we share money, resources and homes with – our parents or caregivers being the first and most formative. That we then rarely talk about money means what we learn as children is rarely challenged throughout our adult lives, so we might assume that the behaviours we learn from our parents are normal.

Often we don't realise that our version of normal is not quite 'normal'. I used to live entirely in my overdraft, and had about three active credit cards, plus one I'd forgotten about. Towards the end of the month I'd make a few phone calls to add up what I had left to spend on my cards. I saw 'available credit' not as more debt, but as my money to spend. I genuinely didn't understand why everyone wasn't borrowing as much money as possible. When I said 'I'm skint' I meant I absolutely cannot access any more cash this month, yet when friends said it, they probably meant 'I am not dipping into my savings for that.' I was very comfortable with debt. It's not abnormal, but it isn't normal either.

It's often suggested that the basics of personal finances should be added to the curriculum and taught at school. It probably would be more beneficial to learn about budgeting and compound interest than how oxbow lakes are formed.

If schools taught us about healthy personal finances then at least we would be armed with the right terminology and have a vague knowledge of what we should be doing, even if we chose not to. But the fact is they don't, and some experts believe it would be pointless if they did since, as with healthy eating or exercise, what is practised by those around us is often far more influential than structured lessons.

Which is not to say that all issues with money can be tied back neatly to a parent who was bad with money – some financial issues are more complicated, but still take root in childhood. One financial therapist told me of their client, a 38-year-old woman called Nieve who was experiencing high money-anxiety. Nieve had 'surprise' tax bills she hadn't put money aside for, and never knew if she and her boyfriend, whom she shared a joint account with, were in debt or in credit. Her boyfriend readily admitted he was bad with money.

Nieve said she hadn't learned anything about money from her parents, 'Nothing. It was impolite in my family for girls to discuss money. Girls aren't meant to worry about it; the men take care of it all.' Imagine trying to gain control over your money when you share an account with a boyfriend who admits they're reckless with it, but deep in your psyche you believe a man will sort everything out. Working with her financial therapist Nieve unpicked these contradictions and realised that it was down to her to take control. She had to assert the power she had rather than wait for a man to sort out the finances.

Nieve won't be the only woman who learned that 'money is a man's thing' from her parents. In 1984 only 57 per cent of mothers with children over five years old worked, which means that over a third of millennials had full time 'stay at home' mums. No matter if equality was taught in theory, gendered roles were modelled at home. The majority of the workforce currently fighting for equal pay grew up in homes where the man out earned the woman by default and research shows the gender pay gap starts early with boys getting on average 20 per cent more pocket money than girls.

I asked Thomas Faupl, a leading financial therapist in the US, to explain in broad strokes how our parents and our childhoods affect our relationship with money as adults. 'Kids are like sponges. They internalise experiences growing up. Our beliefs, our behaviours and even our fantasies around money are rooted in our societal conditioning from the culture and class of those we grew up around.' It's really hard to escape what we learn when we're young; just as children have a magic ability to learn a foreign language, things like 'haircuts are a waste of money' or 'retail is therapy' get hardwired into us.

What is money for? Many adults probably can't articulate their answer to this question. It's a difficult one – do you believe money is for security, or fun, or to impress other people? Is what you earn your complete identity or just something that is needed to get by? Our core beliefs about money are formed way before we earn our first pay packet. As Thomas says, 'Perhaps money was something to be competitive about with the neighbours. If money was seen as a status symbol and it was all about having the latest car or trainers, all of that is remembered by the child too.' So it's not just about actions or habits being passed down, like how to tip or when to save; we also absorb big concepts like the value of money: whether it is good or bad, whether rich people should be admired or mistrusted and whether poor people are virtuous or chavvy.

As Brad Klontz, a leading American financial therapist, says, 'Our exposure to diverse perspectives on money is often limited, since we tend to hang around those with similar beliefs and financial status. As a result, our [beliefs] are often based on partial truths about other groups, and are rarely challenged.' Importantly, these beliefs and ideas – no matter how uninformed they are – will affect our earning potential as we get older. 'If you believe rich people are greedy – even subconsciously – you're probably not going to try to become rich.'

We know wealth and privilege are often passed down through inheritance and the Bank of Mum and Dad. But what we don't often think about is how attitudes towards earning and spending and levels of financial literacy are also passed down from generation to generation. As Thomas told me, 'if you grow up in a family where there is no major crisis around money and there is good modelling around it, where your parents sit down and say, "Here is a little job to earn some money", and "This is what you should do with it", "This is how you save", "Let's get you a saving account" – well you'll probably have a healthy relationship with money, an objective one.'

Being taught how to invest, how to make the most of your money, even how to budget, is another form of inheritance. We copy good habits as much as we replicate the bad ones.

Although it's not always as linear as repeating what our caregivers did with money. What we experience as children doesn't affect every adult in the same way. Thomas tells me about one of his clients: 'This guy had run up $50k in credit card debt and not told his partner. But he had grown up very poor, [and] sometimes people who grow up poor live large in life because the deprivation they experienced in childhood was so painful and so difficult that they are going to live another life whether they can afford it or not.'

We all know those moments from childhood, the ones that cut so deep that we hate to revisit them. Thinking of these you can see why Thomas's client used credit to rebel against his upbringing.

Alternatively, if you grew up without much money you might always find it difficult to spend because it's ingrained into you that money is a finite resource. I have a friend, Anna, who, like Thomas's client, lived in a family where money was tight. Anna's dad wouldn't put the heating on in their family home. It was an old building, and he said the heat would just go out the windows. The other day Anna was moaning about her flat being freezing. I asked her, 'Is your heating broken?' 'No, but putting the heating on costs a fortune.' Even now, fifteen years after moving out of the family home, she still economises on heating in a way that her salary doesn't necessitate. Anna lives in a small, modern flat that would be relatively cheap to heat and for which she has the money to do so, but she's never challenged what she learned from her dad. Another friend tells me how her mum warned her to never have a bath when she stayed at someone else's house because hot water cost so much money, and even now she finds she can't bring herself to have a bath at her in-laws.

Feeling shame and embarrassment as a child can make us determined to not feel it again as an adult. One 28-year-old woman, Geri, told me, 'my mum was such an opportunist, if there were free drinks going she'd have them. If she could get away with not paying for something she would. I was always really embarrassed when it felt like she wasn't paying her way when we were out with other families. Or she'd be drunk enough to think we could wander off from a bar but we'd be called back. Now I can't bear to be seen as tight or "a chancer", so I go overboard and often end up offering to pay for all the drinks, or offering to put the whole meal on my credit card when really I can't afford it.'

After talking to many financial therapists I thought I was well versed in all the things parents do that cause their children to have sketchy relationships with money, but it was Jennifer Dunkle, another American financial therapist, who first opened my eyes to the problem of parents being too nice: 'In the last thirty-five years parents have become very attentive, and as involved parents they do a lot for their kids. I saw one mum recently who would give her daughter her credit card for emergencies, but then the daughter would wildly overspend on it. The mum would complain and chastise her daughter, but then time would go by and the mum would give her the credit card again. I see that a lot, where parents have enabled their children and teenagers but continue to help them once they are young adults. It gets in the way of them maturing and becoming self-sufficient.'

I spoke to a financial advisor to the mega-wealthy (people who are worth over £100m), and he told me that the biggest stress for someone at that level of wealth is the effect it has on their children: 'They will always get bailed out no matter what they do wrong, so they often do really unadvisable things.' In fact, a report conducted by Arizona State University, which studied two groups of students, found that privileged kids were more likely to develop addictions to alcohol, cannabis, cocaine and ecstasy compared to national norms.

Another mistake many of us make is repeating our parents' behaviour without considering how our lives differ from theirs. Like Anna and her resistance to heating, I definitely picked up habits from my parents. For instance, I had a very loose relationship with credit that came from watching my mum's generation spend on plastic. I know it was often a balance transfer and a new 0% credit card that meant we could fly Easyjet to Greece. As a young adult I adopted the same approach, signed up for an Egg card and always took the whole overdraft I was offered, but unlike my mum I didn't have a house with a huge appreciating value (helps if you got on to the property ladder in the 1970s). A baby boomer using credit when they have assets of value is very different to a young professional on a graduate wage racking up thousands in debt. I was copying another generation's behaviour while living in a very different time.

I've started to talk about money with both my parents recently. They're divorced, so it's separate conversations, and both have been interesting. Seeing the truth of my mum and dad's pensions is sobering. Had I not written this book, I doubt that I would have asked either of them what they live off now. They were both teachers, so in addition to their state pensions they receive an occupational pension, which makes a huge difference, but still it's not a lot, and it makes me realise I must pay attention to my non-existent pension (but we'll come to that later). Opening up the conversation with my mum and dad, I could feel us becoming more receptive to learning from each other. And coming from a different generation, they call bullshit on things that have set as beliefs in my head – my mum is insistent that I can get married for far less than she sees my friends spending on their weddings, and I think she might be right.

Ask yourself what you learned from your childhood about money. For me money has always meant fun. It was never discussed in my house unless money had just come in and we could go on holiday or pick what we wanted around the supermarket. I totally understand why my parents didn't involve me in conversations about money stresses or financial planning, but it did mean that the only conversations I had around it were about frivolity. Have a think about your own biases, perceptions and behaviours around money and where they might have come from.

Parents might be the root of all our neuroses. But they also nudge us in the right direction, teach us to be rightly outraged by the price of 'local' organic honey and question whether we really need more than one winter coat. Chatting about money with someone from a different generation also makes you realise how influenced we can be by our friends, our colleagues, Instagram and the couple next door. If you're lucky enough to still have your mum, your dad or your care-givers around, start talking to them – at the very least it will give you someone to blame for your aversion to saving or your deli addiction. Just don't let them see your Uber account. Never let them see that.

6

My weird spending habits ...
and yours

Why do we convince ourselves a Domino's pizza is OK but that we can't afford branded ketchup? Why are we scared of looking at our bank balance? Why are you always the first person to put your card down at the bar? Can shopping really heal a broken heart? How does the purchasing of a book we're never going to read make us feel better? Why did you buy a stranger dinner in KFC last night? We all have weird and ridiculous spending habits that can be unfathomable even to ourselves. Money is messy and complicated, and we contradict our own rules in how we spend it. From rent to cling film it all adds up, and it's time we were honest with ourselves about when and why we spend.

I used to set my wall clock five minutes fast so I was never late. Which is obviously ridiculous, because I knew I had set it five minutes ahead, and yet it worked, until it didn't. You start second-guessing every clock and then they all make you late. I employed similar sorcery with money: I'd put a pair of jeans on my credit card and kid myself that I had spent no money that day, because, you know, my credit card doesn't count. Some days Amazon didn't count; that pencil sharpener-shaped spiraliser definitely didn't count. Written down it sounds ridiculous, doesn't it? Some people trick themselves in a good way. They have apps that round up all purchases to the nearest pound so that when they buy a coffee for £2.50, £3 comes out of their account and 50p goes into a savings pot. Why did my denial only serve to punish me? I never tricked myself into good behaviour, just the over-spending, consuming kind.

For all of my twenties I swung messily between shame and denial when it came to money. I never checked my bank account and it would take my card being declined for me to know I'd run out of money. I had bailiffs break into my flat and change my gas meter to a pay-as-you-go one because I took pride in never opening a letter ever. (I can now tell you that when they type your address out in red you really should open that letter.) I know what it's like to be sitting in a taxi as you realise you have no money in your wallet or your bank account to pay for it. I never once added up how much I spent on alcohol. If I was to describe my 20-year-old self's attitude to money in a couple of adjectives, they would be 'flippant' and 'avoidant'.

By the end of my twenties I was earning a very decent amount, about £90k. I existed in such a bubble that I had no idea it was a large amount. I was surrounded by people who earned more than me, or at least they were who I compared myself to. It's amazing how we notice all the things other people have that we can't afford, rather than focusing on the things we're privileged to have.

Because I was so haphazard with my spending, my life didn't feel rich, it just felt full of stuff: Amazon boxes, gadgets with no cables, jeans that didn't quite fit and dirty dry-clean-only clothes. I never budgeted or planned how to spend. Money just plugged holes I created. I'd quickly buy a new pair of trainers I didn't particularly like because I'd left mine at home and there was a lunchtime run at work. I'd commute across London in a cab because I was always late. It was almost like I gave money no value. It was just something to churn through until it was replaced at the end of the month.

I was so money-avoidant that even thinking about it was awkward. I had some rules and boundaries as to how I spent money, it's just they weren't based on sums or even on the kind of life I wanted to live. I'd walk round the supermarket trying to save money, not buying the passion fruit yoghurt I liked because at £4 that seemed extortionate, but the very next day I'd drop £30 on some cold noodles and a couple of beers with work colleagues about whom I was ambivalent. I'd say no to going to Lisbon with some best friends because the flights seemed expensive, but then would consistently smash through £60 on very average nights out. There was no prioritising when it came to spending my time or money with the people I loved, doing things I enjoyed. That's what happens when you are money-avoidant; you just bumble through life buying the things you come across rather than saving for the things you really want.

I also couldn't bring myself to buy anything that didn't give me immediate satisfaction. I spent a year sleeping on a mattress on the floor because I'd heard beds took two months to arrive, and whenever I logged on to IKEA or scrolled through the John Lewis website I would convince myself I couldn't afford a bed, but really I couldn't bring myself to hand over money for something that wasn't going to reward me immediately. I'd go and buy a pair of Acne boots instead. It sounds ridiculous but it took me a long time to realise my spending habits were keeping me trapped in a stressful full-time job. You would think because I worked really hard for the money I would have respected it but I didn't.

Then something happened: I had a baby. When I went back to work I realised I sometimes went four whole days without seeing him awake, so I changed career and took a job at a magazine. It was a dream job, in that I'd get to write and work a nine-day fortnight. But it paid less than half as much as my previous job. When I realised that my salary was about to halve I did something I'd never done in my whole life. I worked out a budget. That budget changed everything. I expected to be poorer. I thought I was saying goodbye to new clothes and meals out. But something happened that I never expected – earning less meant I had nicer clothes and better holidays. It allowed me to swap debt for a savings account, and I learned to enjoy spending more than ever. It turns out that if you think about and plan how to spend, you will buy better things and you don't purchase crap. How I wish I'd learned to budget when I was earning lots.

I'm putting my spending habits here not because I think they're wildly interesting but because I meet so many people who believe assessing how they spend and putting themselves on a budget will make their lives boring and hard. Yet I've never spoken to anyone who has taken charge of their spending and regretted it.

'But I don't want to be told to stop buying M&S microwave meals,' my friend tells me. I'm encouraging her to take up her company's offer of free financial advice, but she's not into the idea. I know how she feels; I was always under the impression that budgeting, or even having to think about how I spent my money, would feel restrictive and boring. I also didn't want the obvious pointed out: that I was spending like a child. No one wants to feel told off. And I didn't want to face other personality quirks that affected my bank balance – that I was a people pleaser who couldn't say no to a social occasion, which would mean I'd attend two brunches on a Sunday, enjoying neither of them properly and spending double the money.

While I'm trying to find the words to convince my friend that facing your finances can be liberating, another friend shares the words that made him reassess his own spending – when a sassy financial advisor looked at his bank statements and said, 'That's cute now, but it's not going to be cute when you're 40.' It was that indelible sentence, my friend said, which made him realise that the future was coming and that he should probably start saving for it.

I don't think we all need to see a financial advisor, but I do think we need to be honest about why and how we spend money and ask ourselves a few questions. What is emotionally driving my purchasing? Is my spending healthy? Am I trapping myself?

Simonne Gnessen, the financial therapist, tells me about a woman who was always the first to offer everybody a round of drinks yet was sinking into debt. She didn't believe her friends liked her for who she was, and felt she needed to be the 'generous one'. Once she admitted this to herself she could start to unpick why her self-esteem suffered to the point that she thought money had to fill in gaps of her personality. If you too always have to be the generous one, it's worth working out why. Does it feel too painful to be seen as 'tight' or 'cheap'? Have your friends come to expect you to offer to pay? Is your status tied to being the enabler or the one with money, and if so why is this important to you?

We all need to learn that there are ways to earn and spend other than the one we know. That way we will healthily question our situation and our habits. Even saving can sometimes be unhealthy, as I found out when I spoke to 30-year-old Matthew, who lives at home with his parents and works as a telephone marketer for £8 per hour. I asked him if there was anything he'd like to do that he can't afford to . 'I'd like to go to the Escape Room [an immersive indoor adventure day] in Birmingham,' he told me. I kept questioning why this was something he felt he couldn't spend his money on, especially as he'd told me he didn't pay rent, and since he spoke about the Escape Room with such enthusiasm. I was curious, what was he spending his money on instead? And then he told me, 'I like to save. I have £25k in the bank.' He got more pleasure from having money. He enjoyed feeling its potential far more than he enjoyed spending it. When I asked him what he was saving for, what was an amount he would be happy with, he couldn't tell me – all he knew was that he felt better when he put money in the bank, and that spending was almost painful.

I now understand the pleasure derived from saving (if not to the extreme level of Matthew). Having a couple of months' living costs in the bank in case all freelance work dries up brings me immense contentment – a feeling that no Amazon purchase can compete with. Working out a budget I can actually stick to feels great too. Previously, I would make large payments towards my credit card debt each month, which would make me feel brilliant, but they were unsustainable and left me with no money, so by the end of the month I'd be using credit cards again and be in exactly the same situation as at the start of the month.

When we try to establish control over our spending we often put double the energy into small amounts than we do on saving larger sums. We'll buy the own-brand cheese because it's an easy win and makes us feel like we're on top of things, but then when we're dealing with larger sums we won't think about saving pounds – it's why the same person who will ask for the £2 back that they lent you will simultaneously up their offer on a flat by £10k, because that amount of money feels too abstract to elicit any real control over.

So many of us skitter around unhealthy spending habits without any real grip on what we want out of life. If we can challenge our own unhealthy attitudes towards money and identify unhelpful patterns of behaviour, our money could work for us. If we avoid our bank statements what is it we're scared of knowing? That the money we have doesn't cover the life we want to lead? We know that more money is rarely the answer. We know when we're spending to keep up appearances, or because we have nothing else to do. Let's try to be honest with ourselves.

How to be honest with yourself about money

You can't have a healthy relationship with money if you're not honest with yourself. Answer the questions on the next page to get started. If there's a question that makes you feel uncomfortable, then it's even more important that you try to answer it. They're designed to help you work out how your relationship with money is holding you back. Having a healthy relationship with money isn't as easy as taking a

few practical steps – if it was we'd all do it. Instead it's about understanding the hang-ups, neuroses and emotional baggage that come
with money. It's about creating a self-awareness so you can control
your own decision-making.

- What is your most painful money memory?
- What did money mean to you when you were growing up?
- Was it used to show you love through presents, rewards or
  bribes – or perhaps it was something that caused arguments
  and unhappiness?
- If possible, talk to your parents or siblings about money.
- Ask them how money was when you were growing up. Did they
  feel on top of things? Was how you read the situation as a child
  different to the reality?
- Ask them what they hope you know about money and anything
  they wish they had done.
- Ask them what they think your worst money habit is.
- Get a highlighter and your bank statement.
- What is the purchase you most regret in the last month? Write
  down why you regret it and what you could have spent that
  money on instead.
- How often do you spend money? Over a typical few days jot
  down every time you pay for something (or get Monzo and
  track all spending). You don't need to challenge this just yet,
  but do take note: do you look for a spending hit regularly or are
  you resistant?
- Have you bought something recently that you know you didn't
  need or didn't have the money for? If so, why?

Spend-nothing days

Want to find out why you buy the things you do? Want to understand what spending means to you? Then nominate some days where you don't spend any money.

It was only through spend-nothing days that I learned the things I could very easily live without: pre-sliced veg, Aperol Spritzes, Berocca, take out coffee and Bounce Protein Balls being just some. If it sits next to a till in a shop, you probably don't need it; you just want to buy something.

I realised how often I buy something for the endorphin hit I get from spending, rather than any need or even want for the thing I'm paying for. Spending makes you feel efficient, like you have achieved something.

In contrast, I realised I enjoyed the days I succeeded spending nothing much more than days of reckless spending. Making it a challenge gamified my days, which meant I got my highs from 'winning' rather than from buying till socks.

There is a clarity that comes from less choice. I felt liberated from stuff. That's what everything in the shops became, just 'stuff'. You're choosing not to buy anything rather than feeling like you can't; so there is no assessing what you can and can't afford. And it's a relief not to feel like an audience to shops and their gaudy windows. That's the beauty of opting out of spending completely: you get to pretend you're better than consuming, and you start to really see just how much of our lives are spent consuming.

As well as having a greater appreciation and a much better discernment for the items I brought into my life, I discovered what makes me happy above and beyond the material: long baths, organising my wardrobe, taking the time to make a smoothie, riding my bike. I had to make space in my life to appreciate these things and in doing so learned that money and spending isn't always the salve I need to feel better.

- You will be able to separate need from want. And want from love.
- It's empowering and freeing to know you don't need to spend money on a daily (or hourly) basis.
- You'll save loads of money (obviously).
- You'll appreciate the things you already have.
- It's a good step on a journey to spending mindfully and becoming a conscious consumer.
- Once you've mastered spend-nothing days you'll find even more enjoyment in spending the money you have.

LET'S TALK MONEY AND FRIENDS

When we talk about money we often think about work, salaries and negotiating pay rises, but actually money touches all areas of our lives. So before we start thinking about how to get more money (don't worry, I cover that later) or how to save it (of course I cover that too), I thought we'd talk about how money affects our relationships. Earning more (or less) than your friends, being priced out of a group holiday and how much socialising actually costs are not subjects we discuss easily. But there are tonnes of moments with people we like and even with people we love when money becomes a point of friction, or at least mild unease. So we're going there. Get yourself a cup of tea and make yourself uncomfortable …

7

Talking to friends about money

In writing this book I've spoke to financial advisors, financial therapists and financial gurus. I've chatted to CEOs, founders of banks and bankers. I've had conversations about money with every kind of financial expert, but you know who I've learned the most from? My friends.

Not because they are particularly good with money, or even because they are shining examples of what not to do. The reason that talking to friends about money has been so enlightening is because I know them and they know me. I know if they're sleepers or morning people, I know whether they are actually vegetarian or just say they're vegetarian. I know if they can pack a dishwasher well and if they still speak to their exes. This intimate knowledge of their lives means that when a friend who doesn't own a Hoover and lives in a flat share where plants go to die tells me that he's recently started paying into a pension and it wasn't that hard to set up, that the paperwork didn't kill him and he doesn't miss the money, well I know it's something I could probably do too (so I did). During my life at least ten finance-y people (and my dad) had told me to pay into a pension, and I'd wilfully ignored them. But one slovenly friend tells me his story and I'm sold.

'I can ask you anything about money now and you have to tell me,' a friend laughs. It's true. In preaching that we should talk about it, I've become that friend, the one who talks about money. They know they can ask me how much to the penny I have in my bank account – they don't, but they know they could. Instead they'll ask me how much money I spent on a creative project to make it happen. Or how much I charged a client per day. They'll ask me what my partner and I spend on childcare for our two-year-old son and then rightly wince when I tell them the answer (£1,248 per month for four days a week, and that's at the cheaper end in London). The questions my friends have started to ask me aren't intrusive for the sake of it, or prying. They know I'm happy to talk about money in actual figures, and hopefully they learn something useful that better informs their own lives and choices.

The most gratifying thing to come out of this new openness is how honest our conversations about life plans have become. I can now be of help to friends when discussing big decisions. My friend Freya was really unhappy in her job as a womenswear buyer for a large London department store, where she was paid £45k. The job wasn't awful but she was miserable; she never got to see her boyfriend, who lived in another city, and she had fallen out of love with the industry, even questioning whether she wanted to encourage consumerism to such a degree every day. Our new openness around money meant she could tell me that she had £9k saved up, which could last her six months if she was exceptionally careful. As friends we could discuss how living so frugally would affect her and weigh it up with how much she hated her job. She spoke about a fear of hers; she knew her parents could never help her out financially, so quitting her job and spending her savings meant she would truly have no security.

This wasn't a conversation my friend and I would have had before I started pushing the money conversation; fears, truths and actual numbers were never part of the chat, and I can feel the depth change in the conversations we're having now. I asked Freya how much she could expect to be paid if she managed to get some freelance work, along with other important questions that I might not have run through before. Together we worked out that there was an alternative to staying in a job she hated. The security of a wage wasn't worth sacrificing her mental health and her relationship with her boyfriend for, especially when she knew that she could get by for a while on her savings and take that time to look for a new job.

Now that Freya had quit that job and was two months into freelancing, I followed up with her to find out how she felt about my prying money questions. By most friendship standards I had definitely pushed the norms of conversation, and I wanted to make sure I hadn't imagined that those chats were helpful. This is what Freya had to say: 'You can get advice from friends, but if you're being obscure about details you're not necessarily going to be able to follow that advice. It's been great being able to lay it all out with you: this is how much savings I have, this is how much my flat costs a month, this is how much I can live off per month. When you asked me how much money I had saved there was a sense of relief in saying out loud "£9k". I'm 34, I don't own a flat and nine grand is all I have left in the world and that's OK. That's OK. It's no longer my own little secret to stress about. It's just a fact.'

I know talking about money has improved my conversations with the people I love and care about, and therefore it's improved my actual life. It's one less emotional burden between us, and on an individual level, the very nature of being open about my own money means I've massively dented any shame I feel about what I earn and how I spend. So, with all these benefits to be had, why don't we talk more about money with our friends?

Well, at this moment in history, our culture doesn't really accommodate people who talk about their money openly. It's still seen as strange, tacky, ungracious, smug, needy and even selfish. A study by Merrill Lynch found that women would rather talk about their own death than their finances. A study by Visa found that women with more empowered views on money – and especially minority, urban and LGBTQI millennials – were more likely to believe in the importance of talking about money. (While both these studies mention women, Starling Bank has found that both men and women find talking about money equally empowering.) We're starting to see the benefits rather than just the awkwardness, but it's baby steps for everyone; we're leaning into the discomfort, not charging at it.

Even I have felt guilty about making my friends feel uncomfortable, and there have definitely been moments with other friends where I feel them cringing and retreating when the subject of this book comes up. 'We've been conditioned to believe that good people don't talk about money. We think "that's what gauche people do",' Dr Eric Dammann, a psychologist specialising in financial counselling, tells me:

'The awkwardness around money is a social construct; it's not awkward because it is intrinsically shameful. At some point it became impolite to talk about our money and that's stuck. Talking about money is absolutely overdue. Sex was once something we were never meant to speak of. Now there is a stronger taboo around money than there is around sex.'

To move culture forward we push against unhelpful societal barriers that stop us living a happy life. Together as a culture we've dismantled many of the discursive barriers that surrounded sex. Any anti-shame movement requires radical acts, like Kiran Gandhi free-bleeding. Right now telling people what you earn and bringing up money in the pub is still a radical act. Sorry to hammer the period metaphor, but I constantly feel like I'm free-bleeding in front of my friends, but every time it's worth it, because it moves the dial forward … ever so slightly.

My friend Al, a 34-year-old guy who lives in East London, tells me he's felt mild regret for joining in a conversation in the pub that I had started about earnings. 'In hindsight I would have been more discreet when discussing my day rate with our (non-freelance) friends that day in the Prince.' I ask him why. 'Because now whenever I go to the bar, it's always, "Drinks are on you yeah?!", and there's lots of chat about "stealing a living", and I guess I feel embarrassed that I do a job I like and I get paid well for it, and I'm not busting my body to do it. I think telling friends how much I got paid, especially people I know earn less than me, lacked tact.'

If the first reason we don't talk about money is because it's just not the done thing, the second reason is that, like Al, we don't want to be reduced to a number.

Sharing the same fear as Al, other friendship groups have

found interesting ways to talk about wages without breaking the social code that says we shouldn't talk about wages. An acquaintance, Ted, 27, who lives in South London and works in advertising, tells me about his: 'We don't talk in pounds, we talk about percentage differences. So my friend got a pay rise and was like, "I got a 20 per cent pay rise." It means we don't judge the amount; 20 per cent might be £2k or it might be £10k. There is kind of an unsaid rule between us, that we don't ever want to lay it all out, and I think it's to protect the person who earns the least, even though I could probably guess to the thousand what he earns.'

One thing that came up a lot in talking to people is that those on less didn't feel they could always share their money worries. 'I just don't want my mates to presume I'm asking for money if I moan about feeling skint,' a young nurse tells me. 'It could feel like I'm compromising our relationship, and I don't want to make them feel awkward, so I never mention it.' Personal finances are the leading cause of anxiety for British people; sharing the details of a stressful situation with a friend could help lessen the anxiety. In July 2018, a study by Starling Bank found people gained more financial confidence from discussing money than from putting money in their savings account. Advice and an ear might actually be worth more than a loan or a gift. This is one of the main reasons we need to learn to talk about money, and all its various implications.

Attitudinal differences can cause as much of a divide as budget differences. Bea, a university student who lives in London with four friends, explained how money judginess comes up a lot with the friends she lives with. 'I came home the other day to find Sarah in the garden smoking with puffy eyes from crying. She'd been home for the weekend and her parents had raised the subject of her reducing her spending and maybe getting a job. She didn't react well and became defensive. I find it really difficult to talk to Sarah about money, because I think she interprets my attempts at advice as patronising. Maybe I am, but her financial situation is a source of frustration for all her friends. Today, for example, the overground from Richmond was cancelled, so she got an Uber all the way back to Caledonian Road. She frequently complains about how little money she has, and then comes home wearing a new outfit. She once had a "breakdown" because she only had £400 left to last her three days.'

As well as creating awkwardness, attitudinal differences can cause real harm to a friendship – so how do you navigate them? Sweeping them under the carpet and judging someone behind their back probably isn't the best tactic. But conversation has to be used carefully. If it's one-sided, with a pre-determined motive, like Bea judging and wanting to advise Sarah, it probably isn't going to create the answers either of them need. 'The intention of the people having the conversation matters,' Dr Eric Dammann tells me. 'In our culture, information about money is powerful and if someone wants to use it to hurt or shame another – for example, showing off about how much they have to demean the other person – well, that isn't going to result in a positive conversation. But if both parties have the other's best interest at heart then great things can come from honest conversation. It's not just about learning from others – really it's that we learn about ourselves through conversation.'

Is it possible to discuss money and not be judgemental? I'd like to think it is, but right now the lack of conversations and sharing around money means we often have a narrow viewpoint on what is right or wrong. There are many other touchy, moral, exposing subjects that I discuss more openly with friends than money. Take Eric Dammann's example of the topic of sex. I've found a way to discuss this with friends and not pass judgement, even though we all have very different sex lives. How is it that a friend can tell me she slept with a guy who has a girlfriend, in the girlfriend's bed, and I can sympathise with her? But when the same friend buys a clutch bag she doesn't need and then moans about being skint I judge her?

With the sex situation, where my friend is evidently doing something wrong and possibly hurting someone else, I can still think positive 'We're all human' thoughts and lend a shoulder to cry on. Yet when it comes to money my brain can immediately leap to a more righteous place, and I can start thinking along the lines of, 'How can you expect sympathy when you act so stupidly?' Judgement seems such a prevailing emotion with money. Remember in *Sex and the City* when Carrie asked Charlotte to lend her money after she could only pull together $1,500 for a down payment on her apartment yet had at least $30k worth of shoes? Those four women discussed everything from anal juice to lost diaphragms and (almost) never judged each other, yet a conversation about money caused the most on-screen controversy and the biggest rift between Carrie and Charlotte. But then Charlotte lent Carrie the money and we saw a deepening to their friendship, a shared understanding of weakness and resilience that they didn't have before. Most importantly, they broke down the judgement that existed between the two of them, not just because Charlotte lent Carrie the money, but because acknowledging money meant they faced and examined the whys of their judgement, rather than allowing it to fester in secrecy.

Evidently money between friends is not an easy conversation, and yes, it risks judgement, offence and embarrassment. But not talking about money also risks judgement, offence and embarrassment. In the absence of actual conversations, there is so much projection. Without the facts, all we have are assumptions, which are often based more on our own biases than reality. Eric agrees: 'The thing is, we learn about ourselves in conversation. Conversation allows us to compute things and work through issues much quicker than if we were to try to get there ourselves.'

How to have a money salon

'What's that?' I hear you ask. Well, it's a drunk rant with a purpose. That first money conversation isn't easy, but it's worth getting through the initial discomfort. I didn't want to advocate for alcohol, but I have to admit that I've noticed this is a conversation that tends to arise at the tail end of a night when we're all a couple of drinks down.

The first money salon I held was with my boyfriend and two male friends. We met with the express reason to talk money. We didn't divulge our actual salaries, but rather talked about everything else: money, our dreams, worries, spending habits, and for the four of us, at that moment in time, that was enough. We found clarity ('Ahh, that's why you broke up with her!'), information ('I'd never thought to book flights that way') and connection ('I do that too!'). Any judgement and shame dissipates when things are said out loud. And like Eric says, you do learn about yourself in conversation. It was during the money salon that I recognised that there are certain expenditures I have a real problem parting with cash for, such as wedding gifts, accommodation and non-alcoholic drinks in bars.

So how to hold your own money salon? It's simple, all you need is: a bottle of wine, three friends, a kitchen table and some crisps and dips for the middle.

Start talking about money and I promise, everyone will follow. Something happens when this topic is opened. Once the tension is released people can't stop themselves from joining in. They might not share exact salaries or figures in their bank account but people will reveal spending plans, revelatory moments and a bit of entertaining gossip on mutual friends.

Some crowd-pleasing topic starters: student loans, who can afford to buy a flat, and that strange thing your ex used to do with his credit card.

Topics you should cover but will require a smidgen of earnestness: paying off debt, what your parents taught you about money, whether you budget and ultimate money goals.

It will be one of the most cathartic conversations you've ever had. Promise.

8

Earning more (or less) than your friends

Well, this is awkward.

Money is a particularly uncomfortable topic between friends. Unlike money between partners, where we're meant to be all, 'What's mine is yours', money with friends is a reciprocal relationship: we have a culture of buying rounds; we split fares on Uber; if you buy the cinema tickets, your friend buys the popcorn; if a friend cooks, you buy something to drink. As relationship therapist Esther Perel puts it, 'Friendship is symmetric. Love is not.'

When I first moved to London from Liverpool's suburbs at age 18, I was invited by a friend to go to his brother's flat for dinner. It was the first time as an adult that I went to another adult's home without my parents. I turned up very much empty-handed. The other guest brought a bottle of wine and a bunch of £1 daffodils. With horror, I immediately realised that's what I was meant to have done.

In those first months at university I met people unlike anyone I'd hung out with before. These new friends called their parents by their first names, bought newspapers and large pots of plain yoghurt and drank cheap red wine that stained their teeth. I'd moved 250 miles and into a different social class. At a friend's birthday party her dad, a Chelsea lawyer, told me a joke he thought I'd find funny: 'What do you call a scouser in a suit?' The answer: 'The defendant!' Navigating a new world was sometimes exciting, mostly stressful and at times painful.

'Everyone has a socio-economic level, or what I call "a financial comfort zone",' says Brad Klontz, founder of the Financial Psychology Institute. 'Generally friends exist in the same financial comfort zone as each other, and what you find is there are certain customs, norms and patterns of behaviour that for the most part a group of friends all abide by: you go to similar restaurants, you buy the same brands, you feed your kids the same things.

'The further you get out of your comfort zone the more stressful it is. It can be small stresses, like not knowing what to do with an extra fork at a restaurant, or what you experienced – not knowing that it was the norm to take a bottle of wine to dinner at someone's house.'

I never want to repeat that experience again. It wasn't just turning up empty-handed, it was the embarrassment at not knowing how to behave. I think about all the 'norms' amongst my friends now, the customs that I know to follow: to ask everyone at the table in the pub if they want a drink when I go to the bar, to say no to someone offering to buy me a drink if they've already bought me one or they're just staying for one, to lend books freely but never ask to borrow money, to split the bill equally unless someone hasn't had drinks … I could go on.

As Brad says, this is how friendship groups work. We socialise with people like us – my friends are of different ethnicities, we have different sexual orientations and were born in different countries, but when I see a group photo taken at a wedding or a birthday party – I can't deny it, we're cut from the same cloth, even down to the length of our trousers. We're so homogeneous I'm almost embarrassed.

You might have a friend who's the odd one out, the scholar of the group or the nerd who never found her gang, but generally we hang out with people who are educated to the same level, who work in similar fields and who – you guessed it – earn similar amounts. Birds of a feather and all that.

In the most idealised version of friendship, money shouldn't be an issue. It's why writing this chapter is the hardest. I don't want my own friends to think I think about money when we're together, and I don't really, probably no more than they do. But friendships aren't just about spending time together and being there for each other, friendships are rooted in activities, in the things we do together, whether it's pints after work or morning yoga classes. Friends share cheese boards and book festivals together. Friendships are all in some way defined by shared experiences, which are in some way defined by our means.

Going on holiday costs money. Going for dinner costs money. No one wants to talk about money, so we just presume what the right amount to spend should be. We can only ever truly understand our own circumstances, and I don't really want my richer friends trying to guess what kind of holiday is in my budget. It's like your mum trying to choose a pair of shoes for you.

We make friends with people because of similarity, but what happens when we begin to diverge financially? As we get older life is teasing my friends and me apart, and our finances no longer look as similar as they once did. Some of us were lucky enough to buy a flat at just the right time, while rent prices are pushing others out of our old stomping ground. Some landed big jobs and others have gone back to university. These decisions, all made on the back of financial means, affect the dynamic of a friendship.

'If you really like your friends and you want to keep them, it's not a very good idea to earn significantly more or less than them.' Brad Klontz goes straight for the jugular, saying the thing nobody wants to hear. Good friendships shouldn't be conditional on drinking together, living on the same street or, dare I say it, financial parity, but unfortunately sometimes they are. Friendships change when circumstances change, when one of you stops drinking, moves to the suburbs or gets a hefty pay rise. Even the glossiest of TV friendships – Joey, Rachel, Ross and the gang – were not immune to issues caused by earning different amounts:

Joey: OK, um, uh, we three feel like, that uh, sometimes you guys don't get that uh, we don't have as much money as you.

Monica: OK.

Ross: I hear ya.

Chandler: We can talk about that.

Phoebe: Well, then ... Let's.

Ross: I, I just never think of money as an issue.

Rachel: That's 'cause you have it.

Ross: That's a good point.

Rachel's point *is* such a good one. It's so easy to be flippant about a pricier restaurant or choosing a negroni on someone else's round when money isn't a worry to you. Having more money changes your version of normal. It becomes normal to order an aperitif before dinner, or to get a cab rather than the bus. Money raises your standard of living and changes your priorities. You get a cab because saving £7 isn't worth the extra twenty minutes the bus will take. Just as to someone earning less, twenty minutes is nothing to save £7.

The other day I met some friends for a Sunday roast. One couple turned up dusty from a site visit to the four-bedroom house they're doing up. After a conversation about brass taps I asked how many bathrooms they had. They had to count them in their heads before they could give me the answer – three bathrooms plus a stand-alone toilet. The two renters at the table must have felt slightly nauseated during a chat where half the group were just listing paint names at each other. We all know being able to recount posh paint names has become some weird class badge that quietly tells the world 'I can paint my own walls.'

I guess this is why Brad thinks friends who earn significantly more or less will drift apart, because spending time together can become uncomfortable. If your friend's biggest stress is how to pay for their house renovation and you're struggling to get this month's rent together, will you feel patronised in conversation with them? 'Different financial means cause micro-stresses between friends that over time add up and can be catastrophic for the friendship.' He gives me an example that basically describes the three bathroom, one toilet conversation I just witnessed. 'Say you start earning significantly more than your friend and you upgrade your house, well does your friend then feel weird about having you over at her house? Do you worry that when she's driving away from your house that she's judging you? These sort of things put tremendous amounts of stress on a relationship over time.'

He makes me think about a woman I know who won't invite her friends over to her flat because she's embarrassed that her parents bought it for her and it's evident that she couldn't have paid for it herself with her charity-sector salary. The wealth she comes from is different to those in her current social circle, and this causes her to feel shame. On the flip side, another woman I spoke to tells me she's never invited friends over because 'my flat is different to my friends'. I'm 35 and still have four flatmates, and I'm lucky if all the light bulbs are working and the cat litter has been changed, never mind posh hand soap and a fruit bowl. I think my friends would be embarrassed for me if they saw where I live, and I don't want that.' For both women the feeling of being different is stopping them from connecting with their friends.

I spoke to many people who describe what Brad called 'micro-stresses' between them and their friends because of different financial means. 'Apart from my boss, only three people know my salary: my mum, my boyfriend and my flatmate, and she only knows because when we filled out the tenancy agreement I had to write it down.' This is Mandy, a producer in a production company. Although she still hangs out with the friends she met at art school, and lives with one of them, as head of a department of a commercial company she out-earns many of them. 'My flatmate was audibly shocked by how much I earned,' Mandy continues. 'She's a best friend but now that she knows my salary it's definitely changed our dynamic, in that I feel she judges how I spend my money, and I now feel I can never say I'm skint or can't afford to do something.'

Sam is a student finishing his law degree at UCL in London. He's from Newcastle and has to work part-time to get by. He's found there to be a huge disparity between the money he has and the money some of the friends he's made in London have. 'There's a social obligation to do things and not mention that it might be too expensive. Like going to festivals and stuff – often people don't appreciate that £200 is a lot for a ticket. Sometimes it's really difficult – especially if three or four friends have already bought tickets for something – to say, "Actually I can't afford that", because it might seem like you don't want to go.' To add to the pressure of keeping up with his friends, Sam also feels his spending is under examination. 'I feel a pressure to be consistent with how I'm spending money, so my friends don't think I'm using money as an excuse to get out of something. If I've said I can't go paintballing for someone's birthday, but then buy myself some shoes for an interview, I feel that I seem hypocritical.' Sam's self-critique sounds exhausting, and I do wonder how long he will last being friends with people where he feels either left out or judged.

Of course, there are other ways of dealing with similar situations – talking honestly about money when it comes to what you can do. 'Me and my friends are very open about money with each other.' I'm talking to Miles, 22 and recently graduated from university in Manchester. 'So when we're planning a night out or doing stuff in the daytime, money always factors into the conversation in a very open way, and we'll only ever do stuff the person with the least amount of money can do.' Miles and his friends' attitude seems remarkably mature, but perhaps this comes from the fact that he and his friends are all in a similar financial situation (recent graduates on graduate wages), and any disparity will be quite small in comparison. As they get older and inevitably one of them earns more than the others, will they manage to maintain this openness? And will they continue to 'level down' to the friend with the least money?

The reality of life is that even if we choose friends because of similar ambitions and taste, at some point we're bound to earn more or less than one of them. I want to disprove Brad and claim that money doesn't come between friends, but as I reach my mid-thirties I can't help but think that it was easier when we were all skint students. There's no denying: it's hard when you're priced out of a group holiday, it's strange when you find yourself judging a friend for buying make-up but never a round of drinks and it's difficult when you feel a friend can't relate to your life. When toxic comparison enters a friendship, it's time to deploy tactics. Can we stop different financial means from destroying a friendship?

'There was a time when I wouldn't have been friends with Shay. She came from money and I didn't.' Fiona, 33, grew up in Portsmouth with not much money, and Shay comes from Somerset and went to private school – but even that description of them is far too simplistic. 'We don't discuss money because I don't think she can really comprehend the kind of money I live on. But I'm glad we're friends and I'm glad I was able to get past the fact that she had money and I didn't, because it's now one of my most dear friendships.' The financial differences between Fiona and Shay existed before they were friends, so their relationship hasn't been contingent on getting over differences but on accepting them in the first place. Even Fiona admits, 'My friendship with Shay made me realise it was my prejudice that stopped us being friends earlier, not her attitude or behaviour. Maybe people with less money need to be more understanding of those who come from money or earn lots. It's really easy to dislike people with more money, people who you presume "have it easy".' Fiona's point is a good one: having money doesn't make you immune to money problems or life's stresses. The dynamic of Fiona and Shay's relationship wouldn't work if it was only Fiona who was allowed to moan. As I listen to Fiona reflect on her friendship, I can't help but think that the world wouldn't be that healthy if we only ever hung out with people who have exactly the same means as ourselves. It's important that friendship continues to cross financial differences, just as it crosses race, class and religious ones.

I ask Brad why we spend so much energy on wealth signifiers that demonstrate to our friends what we have. Brad explains that we aren't always trying to demonstrate what we have with our clothes or what we drive: 'What people are actually doing with signifiers is saying, "I am just like you. I belong in this job, I belong in this neighbourhood." So some of the outward projections are meant to show connection. Something that is very prevalent on the East Coast of the United States is people who have tonnes of money downplay their lifestyle, with the vehicles they drive or the clothes they wear, because that is what everyone else is doing. Whereas on the West Coast of America it's the opposite: people are living above their means and trying to show outward ways of "I fit in" with a much more dramatic way of spending. They want to show off their flashy cars. But both of those behaviours, the East Coast and the West Coast way, are the same thing – they are each saying, "I belong here."'

We all want to be part of a pack, and we want to be loved by our pack. It's why I read the *Guardian* and wear Converse. It's not just what we buy or how we show our wealth that joins us together – it's the movies we watch, the books we like, the values we have. Some of us might go to the cinema, others might wait for the Netflix release – it shouldn't matter.

When talking to the tech CEO, the one earning £200k, I asked him how he dealt with earning so much more than friends. He told me, 'I feel like everybody has a transaction amount that their brain can process without thinking. Mine used to be around £20, and anything over that would take some thought. Now it's around £150; I'll spend that without thinking. I know for some of my friends their amount will be £10. I make a real effort to respect people's amounts.' Another person alert to their own privilege is Keira Knightley. She has a novel way of getting around earning more than her friends, by paying herself a £30k salary, saying 'I think living an [expensive] lifestyle means you can't hang out with people who don't live that lifestyle. It alienates you. Some of my best, most hilarious times have been in the least luxurious places.'

Being conscious of other people's spending limits and not flashing your cash is one side of things, but how do you tackle it if you're the one earning less than your friends? First, be honest with your friends about anything that is out of your comfort zone, and don't get into debt trying to keep up. An early conversation can positively affect plans, but a late one can mar them, so try to get in the WhatsApp group first with a, 'Hey, can we make this Friday an easy one? Come round mine or it's two-for-one in Monroe's.' People will probably be relieved someone has a plan (and a cheap one). Also, and this is important, unless they are horrifically tactless they should be allowed to stress about money or talk to you about a concern, as Alison, an editor in London, said, 'It was a bit weird listening to my best friend moan that her cash offer on a flat had been rejected while we both sat in my tiny rented room. But it was on me to get over that. It would have been weirder if she never mentioned it.'

Brad has studied many groups in different financial brackets, and has consistently found that people feel most comfortable surrounded by people who get them – basically, people who live like them. So I guess Brad is right: money affects friendships. But it's important for our own growth and society as a whole that it's not allowed to affect all of them. Understand that how we behave and our expectations of others are formed by our circumstances. Spend time with people who you like and work through any discomfort with them, because that's what good friendship is, right? Feeling fulfilled in their presence, whether you turn up empty-handed or with a bottle of expensive wine.

How to be a great friend and talk about tricky money situations

Feeling really listened to, especially when it's about something that has been playing on your mind, is such a glorious feeling of relief. But we rarely experience that when it's about something money-related, and often it's something money-related that we're stressed about. Redundancy, getting kicked out of a flat, going through a break-up or just feeling low because of Instagram comparison are all things that will crop up within a friendship group. Wouldn't it be brilliant if your friend felt they could talk to you, and I mean really talk to you, about what they are going through?

Here's some tips on how to have a healthy conversation without skirting around the subject of money.

Listen, don't talk

Radio host Celeste Headlee advises in her TEDx Talk to 'resist talking about yourself'. Don't immediately interject with your own experiences. If your friend says, 'I can't find anywhere affordable to live', don't say, 'I had loads of trouble finding my place too.' Instead listen.

Be a friend, not a judge

In *The Communication Book* Mikael Krogerus and Roman Tschäppeler suggest that you 'resist the impulse of giving the other person advice – unless of course they specifically ask for it. Instead take the conversation back to an exciting important part of the story: "Earlier you said that ..." Take the person away from the smooth surface to deeper levels: "How was it for you, when you ...?" Or encourage the person to keep talking by simply asking: "And what happened next?"'

Money is so loaded with emotion that it's easy to descend into righteousness, or start judging in our heads. But remember, just as judging your friend for their diet isn't helpful, neither is judgement about their finances. Even if your friend has fucked up, what they probably need is a place to vocalise their situation and maybe see for themselves where they are going wrong – hearing yourself speak is a great way to learn about yourself.

Show you're not scared of talking about money

Have you noticed that when something like a pay rise or debt comes up in conversation, people often bat away the details. 'You don't have to tell me what the amount is!' they'll say hurriedly, steering the conversation to safer ground. Don't do this. Instead nod and allow them to keep talking.

Notice the little things

Another great tip from *The Communication Book* is to 'listen out for the details in what they are saying and pick up on these later'. When talking about an uncomfortable subject for the first time, or when going deep on something you normally avoid, there is often a feeling of 'Phew, thank god that is over' afterwards, and we avoid going back there again. Instead remember to follow up. This lets the other person know you were really listening, and that you understand the importance of the conversation.

Take a moment to understand any privilege you have

Recognising your privilege in comparison to others is important for healthy relationships. True empathy comes from understanding that not everyone experiences life as you do. Maybe you're one of the 35 per cent of millennials who were helped on to the property market with help from the Bank of Mum and Dad, perhaps your sexuality makes it that much easier to speak out at work or maybe you've found a job you love – do note that not everyone will be subject to the same environments, benefits and financial resources. If you can take this understanding and turn it into empathy, then you're on your way to much better chats with friends.

Even comfortable friends can fuck up

Your friend might earn more than you, might own a flat you could only dream about and yet still fuck up regularly with money. It's really easy to judge those richer than ourselves for not being good with money. But richer friends might still need money advice. Just because a friend earns more than you, she might still be being paid unfairly for the work she does and need advice on how to speak to her boss.

9

Why splitting the bill is so much more than splitting the bill

Despite what we've told ourselves over and over again, it's really not that difficult to work out what you had at the end of a meal and then split the bill accordingly. The real reason splitting the bill feels so awkward is because it's the moment we have to confront how we feel about money versus how everyone else around the table feels about money.

We avoid money conversations at all costs, but the moment the bill arrives that conversation seems unavoidable. We throw our cards down and say, 'Shall we split it down the middle?' so that we don't have to discuss with friends the relative cost of the fish compared to the burger. What is it that we're afraid of really? What is truly driving the awkwardness? Why do we turn a simple transaction into an anxiety-inducing event?

'I don't want to accept that the experience we've just shared is tied to money,' my cousin tells me. She would always rather pay for everybody than have to discuss the bill with fellow diners. Freud made an observation about his clients that is comparable to the uneasiness we repeatedly feel when splitting the bill: many of his clients were rich, yet he noticed that they had issues paying him. He concluded that this was because of the intimacy of what they had just experienced – talking therapy. They found having to hand over cash at the end of such a personal experience difficult. There is a level of bonding and intimacy that we get from eating with people, and it can feel inappropriate to immediately follow that with a calculation about money. Maybe it's because paying different amounts can feel like a rejection of the idea that it was a shared experience, which has led to 'Let's split it equally' becoming the cultural norm.

Woe betide anyone who tries to go against that grain at the last minute, forcing everyone to get their calculators out. 'If you plan to go against a cultural norm, it can be better to work out details up front, at the start of the meal,' Brad Klontz says. And that's the point, isn't it: none of this would be so excruciating if we didn't have the cultural expectation of splitting the bill evenly. But is it just a British politeness thing? Every culture has a specific way of splitting the bill. Brad lives in Hawaii, which, he tells me, 'has a very Asian culture. The cultural norm here is, "I pay this time, you pay next time", but the agreement is unspoken. I say "I've got it", and the other person makes a mental note and pays next time. But my wife, she went to school on the mainland in the US, and when she first got there she would say "I'll pay", but no one ever reciprocated. People just thought she was rich! It took weeks until she realised no one was going to buy her lunch for her. Finally she realised that it was a different cultural norm.'

My friend talks about how dining out in Rome with Italians was a revelation: 'Conversation didn't break, everyone just threw their cards down. I liked how seamless it was. The intimacy was preserved.'

I spoke to Helen Russell, author of the brilliant *The Year of Living Danishly*, in which she chronicled her move from London to a rural town in Denmark, and asked her if the Danes did bill-splitting any differently from the British. 'If you go out for a meal with friends, when paying, you either go up and pay for just your own or the server charges you for what you have had, so there is never an awkward splitting of the bill. Going out is so expensive, and people know it is such a treat that they make paying easy and fair.'

The Danish method with the server taking all responsibility sounds pretty chilled for every diner, the Hawaiian way sounds as fraught with imbalance and social anxiety as splitting the bill equally, and as for my friend's experience eating with Italians in Rome, well it only feels that easy if there's financial parity within the group.

The British cultural norm is to split the bill evenly and to try to all vaguely eat at a similar level; it's why we often ask each other 'Are we having starters?' as we eye up the menu. But in a world where we're likely to earn different amounts to our friends, and where the cost of living can be really high (hello, London's £5.50 pints), this won't work for everybody. It's interesting that the expense of eating out means Denmark prioritises fairness over avoiding social tension, and I'm left wondering why we don't do this more often.

Some of us don't have the luxury of avoiding money conversations, yet putting our hand up at the end of a meal to say 'I ate less' or 'I didn't drink' can be nerve-racking, and make us feel like the killjoy. Splitting the bill equally also means every diner lacks autonomy. It removes our ability to budget. It puts the whole table at the whim of the most extravagant person. And it's been proven that we spend more when we know we're splitting the bill: a study showed that we spend 36 per cent more money when we know the bill will be split equally than when we know we are only paying for what we had.

'The problem arises when you have different financial comfort zones,' says Brad. 'Splitting the bill works great if you go to a place that you can both equally afford that's right within your budget and you're ordering similar things that cost a similar amount. But problems start to arise if one of you has much more money than the other. Spending habits also make a difference. It's a combination of how much money you each have versus how easily you each spend money. That's where the conflicts arise.'

Splitting the bill, a relatively small calculation, a minor ritual, has become so loaded with negative emotions and it's all because we're trying to pretend that money doesn't matter. And that is just not the case. Even if it doesn't matter to you, it probably matters to someone at the table. As Brad says, 'What's the experience to sit down and watch a friend order an expensive bottle of wine, an appetiser, an expensive meal, a dessert, that you know you can't afford? What is that dining experience like for you? My guess is that it is not an enjoyable experience.'

Brad's words make me think that upfront discussion is the only way to make sure everyone around the table is comfortable, and that money doesn't become such a big sticking point of an intimate evening. The easiest kind of conversation to have is to make sure that where you are dining suits everyone. If you are worried about ending up somewhere too expensive then say something before a place is even decided. 'Let's go to Deedee's, the food is really good and cheap, I can book us a table if everyone is up for it?', is a much easier conversation than speaking out when the bill arrives at a restaurant you knew was out of your price range. Also, only going out when you can afford it rather than accepting every single dinner invitation means quality nights out over many evenings sweating over the bill coming. If you're rich enough that the bill isn't a concern of yours then check with friends that everyone is OK with the restaurant. Be aware of your own privilege, price down to what the person with the least amount of money can afford and try not to mindlessly order wine from the bottom of the list. These conversations will be much easier if you've been open with your friends about salaries and financial situations. Understanding everyone's situation makes group decision-making simpler.

And then for everyone, it helps to accept before you meet friends for dinner that you're not paying for what you eat or drink, you are paying for a night out with friends. Change your mindset about the prices on the menu – you are paying for being served, for conversation, for laughs with your friends. You're not just paying £15 for a burger. The cultural norm of splitting the bill means taking the individual menu prices with a pinch and paying collectively for a joint experience. Even if John did have a Mimosa to start.

How to encourage your friends not to spend money

Your friend WhatsApps you a screen grab of her Zara shopping basket. You message back, 'Get them ALL' and a heart eye emoji. You love your friend, you want her to feel good and encouraging her to buy things is a shorthand way of saying, 'You're great and you deserve to have these things.' But by rooting our compliments in consuming – 'You look great', 'They are totally you' – we blindly encourage friends to shop, and it isn't helpful, especially if we don't know each other's financial situations.

I see enough 'It's the weekend, why not treat yourself?' banner ads that I don't need my friends adding to the cacophony of messages pushing me to spend; if anything I need them to be saying the opposite. When I ask a friend their thoughts on a holiday I'm debating if I can afford to go on, I want a discerning opinion, not a 'just go you only live once'. But we've been so programmed to respond to friends with support that we have to catch ourselves and remember not all words of encouragement are healthy.

How to stop being the 'oh, go *onnnnn*' friend:

- If a friend says, 'I can't come out, I'm skint' respect those words. Don't make them repeat them twice or even five times, or worse go back on them and come out anyway.

- Try to make sure your friend doesn't have to experience FOMO. We can't all be part of everything all of the time, but it doesn't mean it doesn't hurt when money stops us from doing something.

- If a friend shows you trainers they are thinking of buying tell them your honest opinion and ask them sensible questions: do you have something like them already? Can you afford them? What might you be able to buy if you didn't get them? Do you love them?

- Be careful to not make assumptions or blindly encourage consumption with throwaway phrases like 'You should get one' or 'It looks great! Buy it!'

10

Living with friends

Not all friends make good flatmates, and vice versa. Some people want the person they live with to be a best friend who they share a bottle of wine with every night, others want a silent, passing ship and most want something in-between. But finding the perfect flatmates and then keeping a harmonious flatshare is often something that takes a few goes to get right.

We know the stories: passive-aggressive notes left on the fridge, 'I lick my cheese' written on a Post-it stuck to a block of Cheddar. Conversations that start with, 'I don't use the hand soap in the kitchen so won't be contributing to its replacement.' The guy who moves his girlfriend in halfway through the tenancy agreement without thinking to ask everyone else if they fancied a fifth housemate. Living with people is hard, and paying for other people's toilet roll makes it even harder. As Matt Hutchinson from SpareRoom.co.uk, the UK's leading flatshare site told me, 'When you're buying a house it's Location, Location, Location, but when you're moving in with people it's Communication, Communication, Communication.'

Cleaning, noise, money and people's partners are the top four things found to annoy people in flatshares, with 25 per cent of people having had a run-in with a flatmate over toilet roll.

In all my chats about money, of which, you can appreciate, there have been many, it wasn't often that people talked about money in pence. Unless, that is, they were talking about living with others. Like the bottom drawer of a shared fridge, resentment between housemates festers, and 67p suddenly seems like a perfectly reasonable amount to end a friendship over. In my conversations with people who lived in flatshares I soon realised that, the greater the rage of the flatmate, the smaller the offending item was likely to be, from cushions to dishwasher tablets to pubic hair. And pence.

I was privy to so many conversations like this one, between two young professionals who live in a four-person house-share in Bethnal Green, London:

Rebecca: Last year, before I moved in, you were in charge of house bills, and you always used to bitch to me that Rach and Nura would pay like 67p less every month, and it adds up and they don't care …

Jake: It was so annoying. It does add up! Especially if it's every month you're underpaying by a slight amount. And underpaying slightly still means there isn't enough money in the account and the rent bounced once month and then I have to sort out the charges. And it's the messaging people, it's so much time and effort to go through. And it's interesting how it affects relationships, because you start bitching about people for literally 67p. I can't help but think they are lazy and that they don't care, and I wonder, 'Why aren't they checking how much they owe me?'

Rebecca: Rach and Nura would definitely be the two people you'd identify as being in the most comfortable position too. Nura has a Dior backpack. Rach lives in an Uber.

Jake: Well, 67p is nothing to some people, and £7 is probably nothing to Rach and Nura so they don't think about it. They are in such a comfortable financial position that they just wouldn't think how underpaying by 67p would ever affect anything.

I played this tape to my boyfriend and he said, 'I don't relate to that, I was never that petty.' I had to remind him that he used to constantly moan about his flatmate's habit of putting a half-eaten banana back in the fridge for later. Petty is what flatmates excel in.

As SpareRoom Matt says, 'when flatmates have conversations and one person says, "You owe me £6 for toilet roll and toothpaste", you might not know what that conversation means to somebody else, because it's hard to know what money means to some people. A group of housemates will have different levels of income, and something as little as £5 might not mean much to you but can actually mean the difference between getting through the week or not to somebody else, or getting to work that day or not having to eat noodles for a week. And so even if you think somebody is very well off, you never really know. It's important to understand that you don't truly know how someone else will feel when you talk about money.'

Added to this uncertainty is our own inability to approach

the conversation. We haven't developed a casual vocabulary to talk about money, so just the mention of it can feel charged with emotion. What is a chat about milk to one person – 'I bought the teabags and the milk but you haven't give me any money' – isn't just a chat about milk to another, it's an accusation and a personal attack.

The 67p that Rach and Nura underpay Jake every month is a perfect example of how small things become huge between people who share the same front door. 67p can buy you a Mars bar or a pint of milk, it's not going to change your life expectancy, but being 67p down on your rent standing order can also cause the bank to charge you a £25 late payment notice. It can also, as it is to Jake, be emblematic of a lack of respect.

'Getting the admin side of a flatshare correct at the beginning is often as crucial as finding the right people to live with in the first place,' Matt tells me. 'Have an upfront conversation where you discuss possible tension points, like cleaning, bills, parties and other halves. I'm not saying everyone should list everything that could possibly go wrong, but to outline how you all feel about certain things is important – how much someone wants to party, say, or if people want to share items like shower gel. Then make sure the admin is evenly split, so no one person is responsible for everything; somebody might be responsible for the rent, somebody else for the gas bill, somebody else for the council tax, and then just set up standing orders so you pay each other automatically without thinking about it.'

Taking the time at the beginning to think about possible tension points like whether everyone wants a cleaner, whether there will be a kitty for items like dishwasher tablets or if there is anything communal the flat needs, like a toaster, is paramount. Conversations are harder to have once resentment has set in, so have the chats early, before you've started to find each other annoying. As Matt says, 'People often ask us what the best way to deal with arguments in a flatshare is. Our answer is "avoid them in the first place". That might sound a bit flippant, but it's amazing how many issues you can avoid by discussing them up front, preferably before you move in.'

Like toilet roll, late payments came up time and time again, but you know what nobody seemed to be doing about them? Asking the people who are late to stop being late with their payments. Like Romilly, a 25-year-old living in Glasgow: 'Say if Sasha hasn't paid her rent into my account in time, I'll just have to pay it from my savings while I wait for her to pay. That happens quite often, but I'd rather do that than get all stressy and be like, "Please can you pay it right now?".' Or Dan, a 26-year-old living in Chepstow, near Bristol, 'I'll do the initial text, then I'll leave it a bit before my second prompt and hope that they remember. I would never ask for it face to face even though we see each other most mornings.' Or Amie, 23, in a flatshare in Finsbury Park, London: 'If I have to chase my flatmate on late payments I'll make it really jokey and chilled to mask the awkwardness, like, "Can you send the $$$ please babes" or something.' So how should you remind someone about a late payment? Pre-empting the payment date is a good idea, then you can pitch it as a reminder for everyone, 'Rent is due next Tuesday. Please make sure it's in by Monday to avoid charges.' If you're the person who every month has to be reminded then take a moment to set all your standing orders up correctly. It doesn't take long: ten minutes, a phone and your flatmate's bank details are all you need. Do it properly once and you can save yourself an uncomfortable conversation every single month.

There is a lot to be said for keeping money between the people you live with transactional. If you can't get over the awkwardness of money conversations with friends, then another option is to live with strangers, and actually, SpareRoom often find that people prefer to live with flatmates they've never met rather than a friend they've known for a while. 'I'm not embarrassed to ask people for money because it's just admin and I don't want my flatmates to be embarrassed to ask me if I owe them money and I've forgotten. I would want them to tell me.' Claire only met her flatmates when she moved in with them, and her easy attitude to discussing money with them backs up Spare-Room's findings. With strangers admin is admin, yet with friends it has a far greater potential to become emotional and charged.

But whether you're friends or strangers, wildly different expectations can still cause rifts. 'When you're trying to save money, you don't think you have to buy a new kitchen sponge. You don't even think about it. But if everyone had the same attitude the house would be a shithole.' I hadn't anticipated the rant I would be met with when I asked Leila about her flatmates. Leila, 30, is a production designer living in North London in a shared house with her boyfriend and one other guy. She says her flatmate always says he doesn't have money to buy basics around the house but then will order a takeout pizza. I don't know Leila's flatmate and am meeting Leila for the first time so I can't judge if the issue is about money, respect or just different standards of cleanliness and tidiness. She says 'it can annoy me when he sits on the cushions I bought for the house. I just feel he doesn't contribute to the house feeling like a home, and doesn't respect or even realise the money and the time I put into it being one. Oh and another thing! I buy the twelve-pack of toilet roll because I shop online, yet my flatmate only ever buys toilet roll when it runs out, and he'll run to the corner shop and buy a two-pack and then think he's done his bit and it's my turn to buy the toilet roll again.'

It sounds obvious, but people often fail to see that what they class as standard, others class as luxuries. I have sympathy for both Leila and her flatmate. Making the house feel warm and inviting is important to her, but to her flatmate being able to chill with a takeout pizza is more important than contributing to a cushion. Expecting everyone to want to chip in to something you see as standard, like Sky Sports or a cleaner, is a bold move. Being mindful of the group and where you sit within it is important. Perhaps Leila would have a better time accepting that she is the homemaker of the flat rather than trying to bring everyone else along on her cushion-plumping crusade. And perhaps her flatmate should chip in to her online shop, or just buy a twelve-pack of toilet roll if he really wants an easy life.

Different money attitudes can drive flatmates apart. But unfortunately someone's issues around money might not be something you see unless you go on holiday or live together, and then it's too late. Charlie and Claire had been friends since university, and were close. When they both moved to London at age 25 they decided to move in together, but the blissful flatshare never quite happened. Money came between them, and it wasn't because they spent money differently, or had more or less than each other; it was their attitude to risk and responsibility. I heard Claire's side of the story. 'Two things only occurred to me once we'd been living together a short while: one, I didn't know what Charlie was like with money before we decided to move in together and I hadn't thought to check, and two, I had no idea how much coaching she needed over the simplest of life admin.' Charlie and Claire's relationship was tested through unpaid gas bills and small incidents like keys accidently left in the front door overnight. 'In the end it became frosty. I couldn't bear to ask her to pay for something she had forgotten about, and I couldn't ever leave her to sort out anything for the house because I knew it wouldn't happen. The sad thing is, Charlie was fairly breezy about it all. I'd be really stressed that we had a red letter threatening court and that didn't stress Charlie out.'

It's easy to get excited about all the fun and possibilities of living with a best friend and forget that living with someone is always accompanied by admin sessions and money chats. A friend you have great nights out with might not be the best person to load a dishwasher with.

Just because you have different attitudes doesn't mean it can't work out. It's all about respecting (and sometimes tolerating) differences. As Danny, who now lives with his wife, found during his flatshare days, 'there can be a good side to living with people who count pennies ... Having a flatmate obsessed with saving money was a pain in the ass when it came to his rants about why it was more economical to buy the expensive washing-up liquid (more washes per bottle apparently). But then he did obsessively change our energy providers and would sign us up to free trials for subscription

TV when huge sports tournaments were on and actually remember to cancel them when the tournament finished. He'd also be all over things like Giffgaff way before anyone else and tell you exactly which plan to go for, so I can thank him for my £12 monthly phone bill.'

Perhaps you're reading this thinking, 'that bill-swapper guy sounds like a gent', or like me you hear that and think, 'we would have made terrible flatmates together'. Does Leila sound like a nightmare vigilant housemate, or does her flatmate, the guy who never buys a kitchen sponge, sound awful? I always hated it when a flatmate would ask if I wanted to go halves on a wok and I'd be thinking, 'I'd much rather buy a new shirt.' We all have such different attitudes to household responsibilities, different personal boundaries, different incomes and priorities. It's important not to expect people to be just like you, and to try to respect how they live. Also, something we should all consider is how our own behaviour or even expectations are affecting the harmony. What you consider standard – like pouring Toilet Duck around the rim of the toilet every night – might be extreme to someone else.

We become petty about money in a flatshare not because 67p really matters to us, but because it gives us something tangible to focus our frustration on. When our living space is being compromised small things become huge, and pettiness is often a way of trying to find control in an uncontrollable situation. At the end of my interview with SpareRoom Matt, after we'd covered all the toilet roll and admin chats, he said, 'just one thing that I think is really important. We all have a friend who never buys a drink but having a drink is never quite the same without them there. Sometimes it's hard to quantify what exactly someone brings to a friendship group or a flatshare, but it's important to remember that not everything can be brought down to tangible contribution. I think a certain amount of realism that not everyone in a flatshare is going to contribute equal amounts and not everyone is going to be best friends is useful. Also understanding that whatever is really bothering you, the other person probably isn't doing intentionally – even forgetting to pay money they owe you. They probably did just forget to pay and have no idea you've been stewing over it for weeks.'

Neutralising conversations about money to be just that – boring admin chats, rather than emotional hand grenades – seems more important with people you live with than any of your other relationships. If you have the right conversations early on, have them properly and take them seriously, then there's a small chance you'll only have to have them once. And wouldn't that be lovely?

The answer to a comfortable flatshare lies in weighing up the emotional stress of a conversation about toilet roll with the price of toilet roll. It's about having brave conversations before you move in together. It's about checking you have similar expectations of each other and of the flat. It's about modelling the behaviour you want from the other person rather than stooping to the lowest level of pettiness in the flat. There is far more pleasure to be gained from thinking you are doing it right, rather than trying to do it wrong because other people are. Living with people is really hard, so expect it to be hard from the outset. If they are not your people, if you fundamentally have different ways of living, then look to live with other people – just don't expect them to be any better! If all your flatshares feel like hell, consider that you might be the problem flatmate. Don't let 67p and half a banana defeat you. Plump those cushions with pride, and don't invite your boyfriend to live with you without checking with the rest of the flat first.

11

The problem with hen dos, stags and other social obligations

The email or Facebook message is always so casual, even though it inevitably ends with the sort code and account number of a woman you've never met.

She'll be asking you to 'pop' £215 into her account. The money is meant to cover 'the accommodation and all alcohol' for the hen party of a friend you haven't seen in six months. The email also mentions that you might want to bring cash for the pub you'll walk to on the first afternoon, so the £215 doesn't really cover all the alcohol. Then when the dedicated WhatsApp group is in full flow there'll be a 'fun suggestion' from one of the bridesmaids: everyone could buy the bride a pair of knickers as a gift, nice or novelty, it's your choice! And amongst 147 new message notifications the maid of honour will have warned everyone that 'we'll sort the food costs out for the weekend when we're all together'. Can't wait!

When I receive a hen do invite there is a moment in my head when a ten-year friendship is pitted against what will end up being a £400 weekend. Here's the thing about hens and stags and weddings and other people's babies: you can't plan or budget for them. I hate the feeling of my money and my time being held to ransom. It can feel as if all choice has been removed because to say no, you become 'that person'. Passing on a holiday with fourteen strangers who you know only by their dietary requirements and the number of kisses they sign off a WhatsApp with makes you the socially awkward one.

Of the eighteen people invited to the average hen do (which I already think a little brutish in its optimism), some will be excited, but most will be annoyed. The only time I've ever heard hens or stags not moan about the impending 'party' is when a small group of very close friends have used a hen as an excuse to go on a holiday. But as soon as there is a stranger invited, the moaning begins. It's just too difficult to align a group of people (some of whom have never met) on the definition of fun and the right amount to spend on that fun. OK, I will relent – not all hen dos are bad. I've been to one before and come back happy, feeling full of conversation, friendship and red wine. But mainly I've survived hen weekends and spent too long in the toilet or trying to find a person who doesn't verbally hashtag sentences.

Despite the many excuses I role play in my head, my intrinsic social need to not be a dick always wins out over my bank balance and mental health, and when the next hen do invite rolls in I inevitably say yes. There is a feeling of power-lessness that comes with each baby shower, hen or stag do invite, and I always give in to it. I don't want to be tight and I don't want to be a killjoy. I also know sometimes everyone being absolutely expected to say yes to a social event can be a really great thing – we all remember the wedding we dreaded attending that turned into the night of our lives.

In 2017 research showed that the average hen or stag do

cost £171 per person. I've also seen research that suggests 2018 hen dos cost an average of £500 per person. That's not an amount I've ever been asked to pay; perhaps there's a couple of hefty Vegas runarounds that have hiked up the average. I normally find I'll be asked for a lump sum, around £200, for accommodation, food and drink, and then there will inevitably be a last-minute request to buy an inflatable, a rounders kit or a bottle of tequila.

The question that needs answering is: why have they become so big? When did three nights in Barcelona become acceptable? Why does it have to be a house in the countryside? Firstly, we have been fed images of bachelor parties on social media, in films and from celebrity friendship groups. We absorb those images and expect our own hen and stag dos to reflect them. This grows into a list of things that must be ticked off: glamorous location, tick; never-ending alcohol, tick; entertainment, tick; personalised merchandise, tick. Secondly, they're a once-in-a-lifetime event – you're not meant to have two hen dos, so there's pressure to get it right. These two things combined mean the person organising has too much inspiration to draw from and no reason to dial it down. Once someone in a group has had a trip abroad planned for them it becomes awkward to make the next one a night in the local pub, so we're backed into a corner where we are constantly trying to outdo the last hen or stag do we went on.

Then there is the wedding itself. Even though the couple getting married fund most of the costs of the day itself, it's still heavy work being a wedding guest. The average price of attending a wedding abroad is estimated to be £2,050, and even ones on home soil range from £400 to £1,050; whichever end of the spectrum you're at, being a guest is not cheap. That the invites come with a request for a present (which I've noticed happening on baby shower invites too) still astounds me, although I guess the absolute honesty of a gift list – you can attend my wedding in exchange for a DeLonghi kettle – is refreshing. They also stop money being wasted on gifts no one wants, or the happy couple ending up with three Le Creuset casserole dishes.

So much is expected of guests. The first and most annoying expectation is that you say yes to any invite. People should be allowed to invite whomever they want to their wedding, whether it's in the church down the road or in Sicily, but it's the guest's prerogative to say no. Right now it's far too weighted on the guest to toe the line or feel the guilt.

So how do we stop someone else's big day from ruining our summer? First, if you're planning a hen or a stag do – dial it back. No one wants to go on a mini holiday they have no control over. Second, I don't want to become a complete fun-killer, but I do want people to feel brave enough to say no to a social obligation that causes them anxiety. I realise it's too easy for a stranger to say 'just don't go' next time you're invited – only you know the true fibres of your friendships and the cost of saying no – but often we dread turning down an invite only to find that the repercussions aren't that bad. No one wants a reluctant guest, so going when your heart isn't in it might be more of a bad friend move than not going. You never know, they might be hoping a few people say no to keep costs down; feeding people wedding food isn't cheap.

Once again the earlier you have the conversation the better. The moment the save the date email goes out for a wedding you're not excited by, you're allowed to say, 'Next summer is already packed for me so I'm afraid I can't make this.' This is about using your money and time in the best possible way. If you spend £1k attending a wedding (which sounds like a ridiculous amount of money, but add up engagement drinks, travel, accommodation, outfit, gift and the bachelor party and it adds up) then it's £1k you're not spending on something you've always wanted to do.

Baby showers and hen and stag dos as we know them aren't traditions that date back decades. They are an industry. When you attend them you're feeding that industry, not a friendship. Of course, there are hen dos and stag dos and weddings that will be absolutely worth the travel, the money and the annoying guy that flew in from Denver, and there will be ones that aren't. My advice to you is to judge each one individually on whether you really want to go, rather than feeling absolutely obliged just because they thought to invite you.

How to bring other people's weddings down to your size

You don't need to buy a new outfit. At a wedding you can always spot the people who have panic-bought new shoes and an awkward asymmetric dress, or hired an ill-fitting suit. The people who look comfortable in their clothes always look best, and they don't have Compeed plasters poking out of the back of their slip-ons either.

- If you don't own a suit you don't have to wear a suit.
- You don't need to buy new underwear for someone else's wedding.
- Control pants are expensive and make it really hard to pee.

- If you don't want to go, remember this: life is short and you will never get 20 July 2019 back again.
- A gift list is merely a suggestion.
- You don't have to stay in the same hotel as everyone else, or get the same train, or drink the same drink.
- The married couple will never know if their confetti was personalised.
- No one needs to attend the stag, the wedding *and* the brunch the next day.
- If you're invited to the evening only then they are giving you an out. Take it!

12

Alcohol, cocaine and other vices

People take drugs. 'Normal' people with jobs and friends and kids take drugs. In London you can get a gram of cocaine delivered quicker than a pizza. If I wanted weed I could take £20 to my local bus stop and I'd be home with a baggy in fifteen minutes. I'm not going to pretend it's not happening. I'm not going to talk about drug use in hushed tones or try to condemn it with every other sentence. There is a taboo surrounding drugs and alcohol that stops us from talking about their use, their consequences (good and bad) and their prevalence, and when we do discuss them the conversation centres on the extreme cases – the heroin addict – or descends into judgement. But drugs are a major part of how some people socialise, and they play an important role at mass cultural moments like festivals, gigs and weekenders. Perhaps you're reading this with a raised eyebrow. But wait, and consider that when judgement wraps itself around a topic it blocks honest conversation. And that means it's pushed to a place where it can't be discussed or examined. It also means people lie to others and to themselves.

Thirty-five per cent of UK adults say they have taken

recreational drugs at least once and 4 per cent of 15–34-year-olds say they've taken cocaine in the last year, but surveying is no way to truly understand the extent of drug use. While self-reported numbers can look low, the sewers tell another story: London's waste water has the second highest cocaine traces found in Europe, above Barcelona and only behind Antwerp, a port city with direct shipping links to South America. There is other evidence of drug use all around us too. London's streets are littered with nitrous oxide 'laughing gas' canisters, and it doesn't take long to catch a whiff of cannabis when walking to the Tube.

'Why don't we just own up to what is actually happening instead of pretending it is not?' asks Dr Adi Jaffe, a world-renowned addiction specialist. 'Only then can we address how we're living our life, and if we don't like it we can talk about doing things to change it. But if we pretend it's not happening then we're left feeling hopeless, because there is a part of our life that is affecting us, yet we haven't even admitted to ourselves that it exists.'

The 'unmentionables' are affecting our bank balance too. Not acknowledging the full extent of our drinking and drug-taking makes it impossible to budget for everything else. If you turn a blind eye to the truth of your drinking and partying, then a weekend just becomes a gaping black hole in your bank balance. You know how it goes: you start the week saying you can't afford a train ticket up to Newcastle to see your family, but by Friday night you're withdrawing £80 from a corner-shop cashpoint that charges you £2.50 for the pleasure. I've never met anyone who says, 'Yeah, I put aside about £200 a month for drugs', but I know plenty of people who spend that amount. If anyone does talk about the amount of money they spend on drugs it tends to be in the past tense: 'Some weeks I was spending a hundred quid.' The emphasis is always on 'was' – only in reflection will someone tally it up. The same seems to go for booze or fags.

Abstinence apps add up what you have saved on alcohol, cigarettes or drugs since stopping. A friend who has just shared her twelve-month sobriety badge on social media told me she's saved £8,320 this last year. 'I've probably saved more, but my app's calculation goes on my guess that I used to spend £160 a week on alcohol, [when] I went out most nights and went large every weekend.' One Year No Beer (OYNB), a project that encourages people to change their relationship with alcohol, cites 'more money in the bank' as a reason to take the OYNB challenge. And the NHS has a 'Quit Now' calculator that tells you how much you'll save weekly, monthly and yearly if you give up smoking. Money is evidently a motivator to quitting drink and cigarettes, but people can drink and smoke for years and never really assess what it's costing them.

On his podcast, Dr Jaffe freely admits he was once a meth addict and that he has previously been incarcerated. Unlike most public figures that have spent time in jail and have been involved with 'the bad drugs' (heroine, crack, meth), Dr Jaffe hasn't renounced alcohol, and neither evangelises being clean nor labels himself an addict. He uses the word 'normal' to describe his drinking now. As someone with a doctorate who thinks about addiction and drug use a lot, and with some personal experience under his belt, I was interested in his thoughts on recreational drug use and whether he thought people acknowledge what it costs them. 'If every

Friday you go out and drink and take cocaine and stay up until 3–4 a.m. and spend the rest of the weekend rolling around and getting your act back together to work and function on Monday, if you have built a life where nothing is happening on a Saturday that you miss and it all works out for you, then that is OK; there is nothing inherently wrong or problematic with that behaviour. But a lot of people will argue, "But what if you didn't do that? What if you didn't drink on a Friday? Your weekend could be full of activities! You could do so much more!" I feel that there is a judgement to that way of thinking; they're saying, "This is what your life should look like. Your job is to get up and to go to the park and to play soccer."'

That's the thing – we're hardly encouraging people to be sensible and accountable about their partying if drinking and drug-taking is always branded as rebellious and irresponsible.

Responsibility could mean being honest with ourselves and acknowledging the cost of partying, both in time and in money. How much is spent on Ubers, off-licence visits, cocaine, pints in the pub, entrance fees, inexplicable purchases of vape pens at 2 a.m., bags of ice, petrol station pastries. Alcohol and drugs lower our inhibitions, our anxiety and stress, and along with the happy, mellow feelings, they increase our impulsivity. Hence the random cash withdrawals and rounds of drinks bought for strangers.

When we're sober, money is often used as a reason to not do things, 'I'm skint so can't afford gym membership, or to go to the theatre / on that family day trip / to therapy.' Yet literally hours after uttering those sentences you're ordering the first Uber of the night, about to voyage across town to who knows where and into god knows what state and come out the other end £80 down if not more. 'I hate looking at my account the morning after drinking,' Tom, a London estate agent, tells me. 'It's embarrassing how much I can end up spending on shots I didn't want. And once I'm a couple of drinks in, there's nothing stopping me from buying all the drinks. I turn into this super-generous guy, when actually I'm quite tight normally.'

I asked Dr Jaffe why people find money for alcohol and drugs when they seemingly can't find the money for other things they probably count as important. He tells me: 'At their core, substances provide us an immediate pay-off. There is immediate gratification, in that they help you cope with the realities of life. They require little work, and are a shortcut to feeling good. They are also relatively consistent, and will provide a similar result every time. If you have six drinks and half a gram, or a spliff, you know the ballpark of where that is going to leave you at the end of it versus going to visit family or going to therapy – those are time-intensive, effortful versions of coping.'

So that's what we're paying for, the guarantee of fun and its immediacy. Despite how inevitable drug use can be, it's not always something people plan for. Unless you're sorting pills for a festival, the whole thirty minutes until delivery that operates in most urban areas means people don't need to think about cocaine until they want it. I spoke to a North London cocaine dealer, S, to ask how his clients bought their drugs. He tells me that while he does have clients who bulk buy, most constantly underestimate their use – 'They'll buy one gram of coke at 8 p.m. and call up again at midnight for another, and they do this every time they buy.'

S tells me about the demographic of his clients: 'Every

kind: builders, bankers, but mostly film-makers, photographers and producers. And mostly men.' Why more men, I ask. 'A woman can say, "Hey, can I have a bump?" yet a man is meant to have sorted himself out.' S tells me, 'Perhaps it's because buying drugs is seen as slightly dangerous and not something a woman should be doing, but really I just think a girl asking for coke on a night out or taking drags on someone else's spliff or taking a cigarette is more socially acceptable than a guy doing the same thing.'

S knows how much each of his customers spends in a month; he's bothered to do the maths that his customers are never going to do: 'For most of them they'd be much better off buying half an ounce of weed for £100 rather than buying a £20 baggy every other day. The way I see it, they're paying for someone else to hold their drugs. And cocaine users, they should just buy a Henry [I had to ask what that is – 3½ grams], rather than buying gram by gram; they'd save money that way.'

This kind of financial maths sounds dangerous for anyone with a chink in their willpower. Buying more drugs than you immediately need will probably just mean you take more drugs than you planned. It's not like taking advantage of a two-for-one deal on dishwasher tablets. You're not going to get drunk, lose your inhibitions and put the dishwasher on all night, but I've seen what happens when people 'stock up' on cocaine – they snort more and spend more than they wanted. As Dr Jaffe says, 'if the use of drugs and the money you spend on them is preventing you from doing other things, because that money should be used for rent or food or taking your boyfriend out for a movie night, [or] if using means you are unable to participate in other things in your life that you want to do, not just things that other people want you to do, I would call that a consequence, and you should start understanding your priorities.'

There is so much truth in the word 'priorities'. I reckon if you sat down most recreational drug users to look at the numbers – especially those who take cocaine (touted as the drug of choice for young professionals because it is conducive to a life where you work five days a week … until it isn't, and costs between £40 and £150 a gram – S sells his for £80) – I would think most would be shocked with the amount they spend.

Although I don't know anyone who hasn't been able to pay their rent because of their Friday night habit, I know many who could live in nicer flats and go on much better holidays – they could fly to Lisbon and back for the price of a night standing in a basement kitchen. 'But they're buying friends, they're buying love,' S tells me. 'They want to be surrounded by people all weekend; to them that's worth the cash.' As Dr Jaffe said, drugs guarantee intimacy. Even if it is a false intimacy that only exists in that moment, it's still hard to put a price on connection and bonding, which is why we allow the costs of a night to escalate: in a way they're priceless.

We'll always find money for the things we really want, but – and this is the real problem – we don't want to admit even to ourselves to wanting some of the things we do: alcohol, drugs and cigarettes. But these are expensive items that mess up our finances if we don't acknowledge them, because we can't budget for anything without budgeting for them.

If people were more honest about the role drugs and alcohol play in our lives, it would take away from some of the escapism they enable. If we admitted why we do drugs and alcohol – to ourselves and our friends – and if we budgeted for them, then we would have to acknowledge the consequences of spending so much money on them. We'd probably realise that sometimes they are entirely worth it, and sometimes they are very much not. I really wish in those few years I was going large most weekends that I'd occasionally put the time and money I spent on partying into making myself happy in other ways. I wish I'd booked a massage. I wish I'd saved. I wish I'd suggested to my friends that we stay in on Friday and on the Saturday get the train to Whitstable and have lunch on the beach instead. The sad thing is, all the things I said 'cost too much' cost less than a night out in East London.

How to not impulse spend on nights out

With alcohol lowering our inhibitions it can be difficult to stick to our own rules when we are drunk. So if you really want to stop spending money you don't have, make it physically hard for yourself – take cash out with you rather than your card.

- Delete Uber, but keep Google Maps (the Night Tube is your friend). If you're worried about having a safe way to get home, get a minicab company's number. Sign out of Deliveroo, so you're not tempted to invite everyone back to yours for pizza.

- If you do become the generous one when you are drunk, try to save those generous urges for when you are sober – that way you can really feel the benefit and perhaps it means you won't feel the need to overcompensate after a few drinks.

- You shouldn't need to buy your friends' affection. If you are always the first to the bar or the enabler of a night out then try the opposite and see how it feels. Let your friend offer to buy the first round.

- You don't always have to be the person who organises the drugs.
- People will not pay you back for drugs the next day. Get the cash on the night.
- You don't aways have to spend money to have more fun. Do you really need another drink to stay dancing? If you're going back to someone's house, a couple of cans of beer might do the trick rather than a pack of cigarettes, bottle of vodka, bag of ice and a mixer.
- If you smoke, drink or take drugs then you can't ignore what they cost. There is no point tracking all your other spending while ignoring these expensive items.

LET'S TALK MONEY AND RELATIONSHIPS

One of the first things people asked me when I said I was writing this book was 'do you and Mark have a joint account?' Money between romantic partners is presumed to be very different to any of our other relationships … for a start you're meant to share. But merging finances isn't always easy – every relationship has two different salaries and two different attitudes to money. With a single 'I do' your debt or your savings will halve. So how to make it harmonious and easy? Let's look at money in relationships from the very first date to the joint mortgage. Whether you're a serial dater, settled down or in the middle of a break-up, we've got all the awkward moments covered.

13

Dating: is it a gender or a money thing?

Through my fingers I watch the moment the bill arrives on an episode of the Channel 4 show *First Dates*. It's a date between a fireman and a Marilyn Monroe look-a-like. Throughout the date he's made a few comments about money, once saying that perhaps they shouldn't order tequila shots as well as the wine they were drinking because 'money doesn't grow on trees'. Marilyn was visibly shocked when he said this, wrinkling her nose and letting out a 'pah!'; I guess she thought it vulgar and tacky to bring up money (on which I'll pass judgement in just a moment). The bill has arrived. It is £136, and she is making no move to do anything about it. He suggests they split it, and she replies flirtatiously, 'I've been hot and fun, come on', almost as if he doesn't understand the rules and she's helpfully explaining them. She then hands over £30 in cash towards the total.

She clearly thought it uncool to bring up money. She didn't want to think about it, because she believed she shouldn't have to. She had pulled off what she believed to be her side of the bargain, having turned up looking 'hot', and she therefore wanted to remain oblivious to the reality of racking up a bill totalling £136.

One Twitter user asked, 'What century does she live in?', and the Internet heaped scorn upon Marilyn, deciding that she was 'entitled', 'sexist' and 'jaded'. Yet in a 2017 survey on love and finances, 78 per cent of anonymous participants said they thought a man should pay on a heterosexual first date, and research carried out in 2018 by the dating app Happn showed that although £70 is the average amount spent on a first date, a man's average spend is £92, whereas a woman's is £47. Watching that car crash of a first date (they decided they didn't want the same things), it's evident that, as the gender binary blurs, the equality war rages and sexualities disrupt the status quo, even in heterosexual relationships, gender can no longer be the only marker for who pays. Right now, there's no protocol.

So what does all this mean for the question of who should pay for what on a date? Should the bill always be split equally? Should the person who chose the venue pay? Or the person who makes the most money? It's not as simple as doing what you might do with friends by just splitting the bill equally, because unlike with friends, a date usually has a greater purpose than just a catch-up. Aside from gender roles, other forces are at work in modern-day dating – sex, power dynamics and tactics.

Let's be honest: we use money and our attitude towards it as tools to get laid. When I asked Matt, a 28-year-old straight guy dating in London, who paid on his most recent dates, he replied: 'Mate, it's all strategy. If I think she's the kind of dolly to appreciate being paid for then I'll scoop up the bill. If I think that might offend her I suggest that we split it.' Full of self-admiration and chat, Matt and his buffed shoulders, zip-up T-shirt and banter could easily slip on to *Love Island*. I listened to him recount many of his successful dates, but what stayed with me was his comment about strategy; how we spend on dates often isn't down to how much or how little money we have, or even whether we're male or female. It's about the impression we want to give. Nico, 26, another straight guy dating in London, told me he splits the bill equally because, 'If I insisted on paying it would come across as weird. Most of the women I go out with would find it a turn-off. They would think I was trying to prove something, and there would be a strange undertone of masculinity to it.'

A date is a high-stake moment. Even if it's a casual meeting, it's still an hour of one-on-one time where you are putting yourself up for judgement. Ultimately most people want to be judged as attractive. Even if you don't feel the other person's vibes, I bet you still want them to think you're hot, smart and normal. We have an innate need for approval, which drives us to want to get it right on a date. I pushed Matt on his 'strategy'. He enjoys dating. He's happy for a date to lead to sex and more dates, but he isn't looking for a relationship. He'll play the role required by each girl to achieve what he sees as a 'successful date' (this might be sex or a second date, depending on the girl), which means his behaviour is malleable. Like his outfit choice and his chat, he knows the restaurant he chooses and whether he pays the bill all build a picture of who he is as a person.

'I pay for everything. It's almost a neurosis. I pay for literally everything.' Walker is a good-looking 32-year-old guy. Is that part of your appeal, I ask. 'It's an easy way to be more appealing,' he replies. 'It works.' Walker takes me through a typical date: 'It's always a restaurant I know, and if I don't know the restaurant I will go first on my own to check it out. When she arrives I'll order two glasses of champagne. I will have pre-planned a cocktail that I think she would like, and I'll order that as an aperitif. Then when it comes to ordering dinner I prefer to have lots of sharing plates, because it's more social, so I always order everything off the starter menu to share for dinner, minus any sloppy pasta, and I'll order a bottle of something with dinner. So that's all the decisions taken care of, which makes the date run smoothly and she doesn't have to think of anything. Then when the bill comes I'm insistent that the date doesn't see the figure at the end because I think that's really vulgar.'

What Walker describes as his perfect date I would find stifling. I find the phrase 'she doesn't have to think of anything' quite problematic. If you actively remove all choices from your date – they don't choose where to eat or even what food and drink is put before them – and then don't allow your date to even see the bill, there's no denying that money is a tool of control. Obviously I'm not the intended audience for Walker's tactics, and I am left wondering, is he extraordinarily controlling or a charmer? I guess it depends who's looking.

'As someone who works and lives in London it's only fair that we share. If one party pays it would change the power dynamic of a relationship.' Gemma, 24, tells me that she pretty much always splits paying for stuff equally on dates. 'I used to work in an office of all women, and there was a girl who had gone on a date with a guy and on their third date he didn't pay for the meal, he split it, and she was like, "That's so rude, I won't see him again." I remember being so shocked that a woman still thought like that.'

Gemma is unusual in being quite gender-neutral in her description of a date – for most of the people I interviewed about dating and money, gender led their answers. No one said, 'If I've just been paid I'll offer to pay' or '£20 is my budget for a date.' Gender norms and roles are so ingrained in our culture that there's no escaping them, even when that is exactly what we are trying to do. When I asked Sophia, a 27-year-old bookkeeper dating in Manchester, how much she spends on dates, like everyone else she couldn't answer without nodding to gender roles: 'I like it when a guy pays. I know some girls don't but I think it's nice. I feel treated. Also dating is expensive! If I let him pay it doesn't bankrupt me.'

Gender was still part of the conversation when I spoke about money and dating with people who identify as gay. Brett, 35, told me, 'I think it has a lot to do with gender still. I see gendered dynamics between gay couples. When an older man with a much younger boyfriend is paying for everything, it's almost like they are role playing the dynamics of a straight couple; they are tapping into make-believe misogyny.' Carla, a 26-year-old woman who dates other women, has a similar experience. 'It depends, but if my date is much older then she pays.' She then laughingly concludes: 'Perhaps age is the new gender?!' It might be, or perhaps it's just a recognition that if you're older you're more likely to earn more money, which is a different kind of fairness. When Brett reflects on it a bit more, he says, 'From what I see around me, a man-on-man relationship is more likely to create fairness, equality and balance. We have an unspoken pact of evenness that I don't always see in my straight friends' relationships, and that

123

tends to start from the first date, with splitting the bill pretty equally.'

Generally we select partners by either 'matching' or 'exchanging'. Matching is when like-for-like pairing is made – two intellectuals getting together or two physically attractive people finding each other. Exchanging is when someone goes for a partner whose qualities they don't have and trades – for instance beauty for status, or money for youth. Obviously this is an oversimplified way of explaining attraction, but it does shed light on how relationships form. Research shows that men who pay for a date have higher expectations of the date leading to sex, which is in some way an exchange. And a male friend recently admitted to me, 'At the moment I'm dating a girl and I'm really punching [up]. She is way out of my league, so as I see it, the least I can do is pay.'

When I was dating, if I ever picked up the tab, by doing that sneaky move of paying for it while my date was in the bathroom, well it was always seen as 'a move'. As a woman I wasn't expected to pay for *everything*. Even when I did it super casually, like paying for the food when ordering at the bar in a pub rather than setting up a tab, it was still seen as flashy or assertive. Yet I was only doing what men on dates with women get to do all the time – avoid a conversation about money by just sorting it. I got bored with having to prompt the 'let's split it' conversation whenever a bill was placed on the table. And, if I'm honest, I liked the control. I wanted to let him know that I didn't need looking after, and to the right man I thought it made me more attractive. It was also a test of sorts: I was weeding out the men who might have felt emasculated by a woman paying.

On a date, money is one of the many things we use to

communicate our intentions: for me it was to reel in a feminist; for others it's a way out. 'If I don't want a second date I tend to pay; that way I don't feel guilty' – when Chris told me this, it suddenly threw a few of the dates I'd been on into a new light. It explained my confusion at a guy insisting on treating me and then ignoring my thank you message: he was using money to diffuse his guilt. By paying, Chris feels he doesn't owe his date anything; he's almost using it as compensation.

What about how much money people have? It seems that tactics and gender norms override our financial situation. 'The amount of money spent on a date is determined by both interest and income,' Wendy Patrick, a psychologist specialising in attraction, tells me. 'Daters who are financially solvent are less likely to correlate the amount they spend to how much they like their date. Daters who are on a budget are more likely to strategically spend to impress, viewing the extra money as an investment in the relationship.' I think about Walker, and how he has the money to date regularly and to put on the same date for every girl. One woman told me if she's skint she deletes her dating apps, because 'it's an expensive hobby. I want to feel on form, and if I'm worried about cash and scared my card is going to be declined, I'm not going to be much fun.'

Another guy who had just turned 30 told me how he learned that a good date didn't have to be expensive: 'In my early twenties I thought for a first date you had to pull out all of the stops. I'd book tickets to see the Rolling Stones in Hyde Park or take a girl to an open-air cinema night. I soon saw that those dates weren't leading anywhere; maybe they sent out the wrong message, maybe they were the wrong girls, but either way I learned that I'd rather get to know a girl in a pub than go to loads of effort and expense for someone I don't really know.'

Often we're looking for someone like us. In relationships you're meant to share resources equally, and that's much easier when you both bring similar things to the table. When I was dating I was looking for a match – I didn't think about it as looking for someone who earned the same amount, but I did want the boy to be into the same pubs and have a similar idea of what constituted a fun night out. If my date chose a restaurant I thought was too posh, it was the biggest turn-off. As we saw with friends, we connect easily with people like us, and unfortunately our finances are part of who we are.

For this reason, pretending you have money when you don't is a misguided tactic. Surely it's better to find someone who likes you for you, rather than putting on a pretence? It's cheaper, and less anxiety-inducing too. A friend, Lucy, told me of the first date she went on with her boyfriend of three years: 'Everything about Bobby screamed, "I don't have any money" – his clothes, that we ate a takeout pizza sat on the pavement and took a couple of bottles of beer down to the canal. But it was perfect, and such a nice antidote to the guys who wanted to go somewhere with a white tablecloth.'

Money plays a big part in getting what you want out of a date. How you use it often depends not on how much you have, but rather on the outcome you want. It's used to appear more attractive, as a leveller, a flag for gender equality and a consolation prize. It's used to assert control and demonstrate fairness. There is no right or wrong amount to spend on a date, no right or wrong way to split the cost: really it's about deploying the right tactics with the right person. Now more than ever, you can date your way. Marilyn wasn't wrong to want a man to pay for her, but she was wrong to expect it.

14

Together: the start matters

So you're through the first dates. Now you're 'seeing' someone. You know where they live. You know they eat sandwiches in a slightly idiosyncratic way. When you stay at theirs you still try to brush your teeth before they wake up, and you're not entirely sure of their two brothers' first names. You alternate rounds in the pub and will pick up groceries on the way to theirs. But your conversations about plans are starting to mention dates four weeks in the future. When do you need to talk about money? Do you even need to talk about money at all?

'I think a good time is when you are about to make decisions that affect you both financially. Like booking a holiday together. That gives you a prime opportunity to have a chat about it,' Simonne, the UK's leading financial therapist, advises. 'But rather than making it a "we need to sit down and talk about finances", it can just be an everyday conversation. The more normal you make it, the more normal it will be.'

It's about making sure money isn't a subject you have to avoid. But that doesn't mean it has to have too much power in your relationship, either. To be able to casually suggest dinner somewhere, or discuss attending a wedding in Greece together, or to even bring the person you're seeing in on conversations about you moving jobs or what it will mean if your flatmate moves out, you'll need to start an open dialogue about money. Which is as easy and as hard as learning to walk to the bathroom after sex without feeling self-conscious.

'All emotionally charged conversations require building up credit in the emotional bank account,' Simonne tells me. She's talking about the process of getting to know someone and integrating money conversations into that. Just as you would slowly bring in subjects such as mental health or your difficult relationship with your mum, money and how much or how little you have, how financially secure you feel, the kind of budget you like to live within, how huge your student debt is – all are conversations that at some point you will need to have with someone you love. But when to have them is the difficult judgement call. 'With some people that might happen in the first date through nine hours of talking, with others it might take nine months,' Simonne says. 'It's a personal thing.'

I can clearly remember telling my now long-term boy-friend what I earned. We were both 28, so way past entry-level jobs. We'd been hanging out for a couple of months but had not even had a conversation about exclusivity. Yet our chats stretched across future dreams, being Northerners in London and why I needed a flatmate (because my £2k-a-month rent was crippling me). I shared what I earned, although I didn't tell him about the four credit cards I had on the go. What you are willing to share easily and what feels harder to say out loud is something Simonne advises people to take a moment to reflect on: 'Notice the things that strike shame, the things you're not willing to share, as they are probably the things you most need to address.'

At the time he was freelance, while I worked full-time. It was he who first introduced me to the idea that time was worth more than money. He chose to live in a part of London that at the time was very cheap (Hackney Wick). He would work intensely for a few weeks and then have a few weeks tinkering on his motorbikes (plural) and learning how to build guitars (I never said you wouldn't cringe for us). For him to explain how this lifestyle worked to me, a self-proclaimed wage slave, money had to be part of the conversation. By being upfront we worked out how to date with two different ideas of what money meant – for me that was 'things' and status, and for him it meant time and freedom.

Claire, 29, tells me about her first money chat with her boyfriend: 'Within two weeks of dating a new boy, my car was towed. I was so upset. I need my car for work, so it really was a disaster. I was sobbing so much that I had to explain to him that I didn't have the £250 it was going to cost to get my car back: I'd just paid for a part-time master's and my mum doesn't have spare money. It wasn't the level of detail I'd ever have normally gone in to, but through chatting we worked out how to pull the cash together. He lent me £150 and I jigged something around to get the rest. It was a real bonding experience, and we were always open about money afterwards. Four years later we're still together.'

She found herself in a situation many of us have been in, where she couldn't talk about her emotions honestly without talking about money. When you think of the alternative – suppressing her feelings and lying to someone she wanted to get closer to – admitting the truth seems a no-brainer, yet many of us end up lying to our partners about money. A recent study by the Money Advice Service found that as many as 45 per cent of us do it regularly.

That doesn't seem surprising, since many of us deceive ourselves about money. I have my Uber account synced up with my credit card so I don't see it on my bank statements. Even with financial products like Monzo, Starling and Yolt visualising our expenditure to allow us greater honesty with ourselves (there is no hiding what I spent on groceries last week), we're still on a journey to individual financial accountability, never mind telling someone else and taking into account the emotions of two people. But as Claire saw, lies are no foundation to a healthy relationship, neither with a new partner nor with yourself. By allowing him to see her vulnerable, Claire learned early on that she could rely on her boyfriend in a stressful moment.

How a relationship begins can set the precedent for the rest of the relationship. The earlier we know how our date feels about money, the sooner we know if we can align with them. As Don, a gay 37-year-old man, told me: 'Now that I'm 37, I'm really conscious when dating someone who is six or seven years younger. I don't want "little old me", the person I am used to being, coming to mean something else just because I'm settled in my career and comfortable for no other reason than my age. I don't want that extra shine, I don't want money to be my appeal, I do not want that. I don't want money to put me in the role of caretaker.'

Don's issue is an age-old dilemma. He wants to be loved for who he is, not for the money he has. I took Don's issue to financial therapist Eric Dammann. 'Is his concern a lack of authenticity in the relationship? That people won't appreciate him for himself? That's a tough one because there are people looking for exactly what he describes, to be looked after. It's a familiar struggle – lots of famous and wealthy people have the same problem. People are there for the wrong reasons. Unfortunately there is no real answer to it apart from experience. And the only solution is time and learning, being with someone for a while and getting a sense of who the person really is and why they like you.'

It's so hard to override money as a tool of power or control, even if power is not what you want in a relationship. If you have money you have a certain power, and people can be attracted to that.

Don recounts why one of his relationships with a guy eight years his junior didn't work long-term: 'There were signs with George in the early days. He had a slight princess attitude, where once we got comfortable with each other he expected presents and treats. He'd send me a selfie of him in a changing room and when I would reply saying "hot" he would say, "Maybe a little present from Don?" Our relationship ended after a few months, and I'm glad I called it early.'

Don talks about money openly, and never hid his wealth from George. I wondered if this accelerated the end of their relationship? 'Yeah, but only in that it reached the right conclusion quicker.'

Peigh, who even by his own standards is 'rich', tells me what he's learned about the early weeks and months of dating now that he has money, and how this affects the rest of the relationship: 'In the long run me paying for everything can create problems in the quality of the relationship. It creates an imbalance. If you decide to go to a restaurant that is too expensive for them they can't pay their way, and that ultimately means you're not "in it together". I've realised that I have to dial down my lifestyle to make sure I'm not calling all of the shots all the time, because I don't want that. Also I always have in mind the places they can afford to pay, so I deliberately don't pull my card out if I know they can afford to get it, because I know what a kick people get from paying, and I want them to have that kick too.'

But your dates must see what you're doing, I point out. 'Yeah, probably, but I can't change that we have different amounts of money at our disposal. At least this way I'm trying to make it a non-issue.' But you don't discuss it, I enquire. 'I did once with a girlfriend who had a real issue with the fact that I earn more. We used to talk about it and I'd ask, "What do you want? Should we only ever do things that you can afford?" I was happy to do that. But after five months we discussed living together, and she would never feel comfortable living in my house. I'd say to her, "OK, so to live together we have to rent out my house, and pay rent on something that will be more expensive and shitter?" I saw her point of view, but I felt that was a bit too "cutting off your nose to spite yourself". We ended up splitting up; the financial disparity was just too big a deal to her.'

I think about Peigh and his girlfriend and how ultimately she must have felt disempowered, and that he didn't want to have to be so aware of his money all the time. It's interesting that they discussed it but still couldn't find a way to make it work; their money attitudes and hang-ups just went too deep. I followed up with Peigh's ex-girlfriend to ask why she thinks it ended. She told me: 'Ultimately I felt that any success I made happen in my life just wouldn't have lived up to what he had already achieved. And I wanted a relationship where I felt in control and the balance was so out with Peigh – you know if he wanted to move to LA tomorrow he could; if he wanted to buy a car this Saturday he could. He had a freedom that I didn't. I'm glad we chatted honestly from the beginning though. We were constantly trying to find a way to make it work.'

It's why some of us are only comfortable splitting things equally on a first date, and why finding someone who feels like they 'get us' is so important – we want parity in a relationship.

As Simonne says: 'We all have our own baggage. We have our own stories and histories and all kinds of complexities that we've grown up with that drive our habits and behaviours and attitudes towards money. And in a relationship, there are two sets of baggage, two sets of hang-ups, different habits, and on top of that sometimes two different financial situations. So maybe at the start you can share your money stories or deeper questions. How do you feel about money? What drives your attitude towards money? These might come later, they might come quicker, but these conversations are especially important when there is a hang-up or an emotional block. When there is a resistance, those conversations are really important. They might never be needed if everything is fine.'

As Peigh's ex-girlfriend told me, 'Peigh and I had to have full-on conversations early on because I wasn't OK with the situation. With my new boyfriend I've moved in with him and although we know what each other earns and will talk about boring stuff like "should we drive to Cornwall because it's cheaper?" we don't have to talk about money any more than that.'

No one is saying you should be talking about money with

your partner all of the time, but you should be able to talk about money easily when either of you need to – you might want your other half's opinion, or maybe you're making a financial decision together like planning a mini break in Coombe. An honest conversation requires trust, and trust tends to come with time. You don't need to force the money chat, but you absolutely shouldn't avoid one either. If you find that it's too hard to be honest about money then there's either a problem with your relationship, with your partner or with your relationship with money.

15

Together for the long-term

'Entire lives are entwined within a marriage. It isn't just the relationship between the spouses. It is social networks, it's lives of children, it's grandchildren, it's economics,' said relationship therapist Esther Perel in 2018. A long-term relationship means two people coming together to build one life. You sleep on the same sheets, you live in the same house, and though you might drive different cars if one of you is making a packed lunch every morning and the other is wearing Vetements socks it might not feel right. 'For richer or for poorer', you draw from the same financial pot. Yet you won't necessarily both fill the pot at the same rate.

Part of dating is aligning on values, on ambitions and on lifestyle. Over the first few months together you start to build a profile in your head of the life you might lead together, and part of this is the lifestyle you will have as a couple. Will you buy the own-brand cornflakes? Will you choose travel over toys? Education over a loft conversion? How much is reasonable to pay for a dog? We enter relationships with assets and debt, expectations and dreams. Often with little conversation, zero schooling and few role models, two people are expected to align happily and become a singular four-legged economy.

And yet research shows that half of the UK's couples (in a relationship of a year or more) don't know what each other earns. When I spoke to divorce lawyer Melissa Arnold, she told me, 'People often have no idea of their finances as a couple. Surprisingly some people may come to me for advice about a potential separation who have been married in excess of thirty years, and you would think under those circumstances they would know everything about their marital finances, but quite often they don't.' Some people have lived their whole adult lives and never had to think about money because their partner 'looks after them'. But is keeping someone in the dark about a fundamental survival tool really generous and caring? Whether on a first date or thirty years later, perhaps taking financial control really means being financially controlling. It's not hard to picture Walker – who never let his date see the bill or order her own food – divorcing a few decades down the line from a partner who has zero idea of their finances.

Financial infidelity is evidently present in most relationships, as anyone who has ever disposed of the packaging from an online shop and pointed at the new item of clothing in their wardrobe as 'oh that old thing?' knows. But while there are money fibs, there are also catastrophic lies. One in six people are hiding debts from their partner, with one in nine of those having debt of more than £9k. The deception of debt can cut a relationship deep. Not only are there lies involved, but debt of £9k could jeopardise joint assets like your home or car. Understandably, this might make someone want to bury their head further in the sand. But while debt may not always be completely solvable, nor is it a problem that will just disappear.

Billie, a 30-year-old who has recently bought a house in Norfolk with her boyfriend of five years, tells me of their most testing time yet. 'When I received a text from Rick that read, "Hey, we need to talk, I've come home from work early, come back when you can x" I knew it wasn't going to be good, but I had no idea he was about to admit he'd spent £2,500 gambling.' Billie is calm as she looks back, but there is still a level of shock. 'The deception was devastating. Also, the shame of losing money to gambling. That happens to other people. I kept thinking, "We're normal, we don't get addicted to gambling!"' At first they thought this would split them up, 'but because he told me rather than me finding out, the trust wasn't completely shot. It actually became a moment of bonding, as it forced so many conversations between the two of us, especially understanding his lack of money growing up and how that had affected his view of it now.'

Chatting to Billie, I saw that even in the worst circum-stances a money conversation was still a positive experience, that it encouraged them to remember something important: they both came into the relationship with different views, different opinions and different life experiences, and while that can be part of what attracts us to each other, it also affects our relationship with money.

But it's not just lies that need to be addressed; working out the financial dynamic of a relationship is an ongoing journey for every couple. The same issues we see playing out on first dates – equality, gendered roles, parity and fairness – all rear their heads throughout a relationship. If you're in a long-distance relationship and one of you earns way more money, do you still alternate who pays for the flights to spend time together? What's the protocol for buying presents for each other if all of your accounts are shared? Even though the pay gap exists, there are large amounts of women earning more than their partners – who should take on the brunt of childcare?

In any relationship, equality and fairness are constant balancing acts, and really that's what we're all trying to achieve: a partnership where both parties feel fulfilled. So how does anyone do it? 'If I worked the same hours as Grey our relationship wouldn't exist,' Kody tells me. 'He's a chef, and the first five years of his career were placements in restaurants around the world: Hong Kong, Bangkok, Los Angeles, Monaco. We made it work by me giving up my career to follow him, and in return his wages support us both and it works.' That's the bit some couples find difficult; often one person needs the support of the other to go to work every day. If Kody had stayed in her job in retail, they wouldn't spend any time together. They share the finances, they share the emotional responsibility of staying together, but they don't share the workload, and I can't help but wonder, does that cause tension? 'It's old-fashioned, it's a bit strange,' Grey told me. 'I'm glad Kody has started to do a bit of work [website building she can do from anywhere], but this is the only way for me to have a relationship with her and this career, and I want both.'

In the balance of a relationship it's important to remember the other currencies in life. One might fill the financial pot while the other tops up the emotional one. It could be seen that Kody contributes more to the relationship through her selflessness, or that Grey is the only provider, but neither version is how they see it. Equality isn't achieved by each partner bringing exactly the same qualities to the table; instead it's bringing together your differences and similarities to create a fulfilling environment for both of you. Some of us are richer in currencies we can't measure to the decimal point, yet it's harder to define those because they're less tangible than the cold hard cash used to buy an IKEA bedside table or pay the bills with.

But when we bring vastly different things to a relationship, resentment is a constant danger. It's too easy for the person who feels they are giving 'more' – whether that's time, money or energy – to feel it's not 'fair'. Listening to Kody and Grey I can already tell they are fairly open with each other, and check in regularly to make sure the other is still happy with their arrangement. They understand and can articulate their choices, and I wonder if this is part of their harmony. The key thing is to have conversations about money. Financial therapist Eric Dammann says, 'People with different money styles and/or different earnings will absolutely get into trouble if they don't have conversations. The point is that simply by having a conversation things are in the open, and then you can choose to act on them or not. Conversation is often the antidote to resentment.'

It's not just different salaries and different spending habits that we need to talk about; we most likely have different money beliefs too. Like Grey and Kody, Dan and Shazia are another couple whose roles might seem unequal. They live in Bristol and have a five-year-old son. Dan's a freelance writer who is pretty successful; he's published a book, his peers rate him and his salary is about £25k. Shazia runs the UK office of a global tech company. She regularly has to fly to San

Francisco, sometimes India, and occasionally Hong Kong. Her base salary is £80k, plus shares and five-figure bonuses. Because she is often away, Dan does a lot of the work at home: dropping off and picking up their son from school, cooking, house maintenance, and all the usual life admin like putting the car in for service, booking holidays and swapping energy providers.

It's great to see any couple bucking tired gender roles, but it's not always easy being the ones going against the grain. 'Now an obvious consequence to a woman out-earning her husband is that it's a blow to the male ego. That's the story most circulated,' Eric tells me. Yet with this couple, the issue it seems is not how he feels about their wage disparity – it's how *she* feels about it. A few years ago, they were arguing a lot. Shazia would erupt at the smallest thing, and become mean and vicious. As someone who believes in gender equality, it was a tricky thing for her to admit, but she had fallen into old gender stereotypes, and had started to almost disrespect her husband because he wasn't bringing home more money. Consciously the feminist in her would never admit she felt this way, yet almost without realising why, she was picking fights with him.

They talked with a therapist, who helped them unravel what was happening; there was something about her making more money that was triggering old stereotypes in her. Eric has seen this a few times. 'It's not always that men feel weak because they're not earning enough, it's that subconsciously their partners see them as weak and the men are reacting to that.'

Shazia's therapist helped her to become aware of the thought processes driving the emotions. She admitted that when her husband is picking up their child and she's on a plane, she has found herself wishing they had more typical gender roles – that he earned the money. This wish didn't fit with her conscious sense of being an empowered woman, and this was manifesting itself as passive-aggressive arguments; she was trying to bury something that she needed to confront and discuss. As Eric says, 'people often have to rejig how they define what makes "a good provider"; in Shazia's case her husband is a very good provider and partner, in that he looks after their kid and their home and he's there for her, but when she was stuck in the old money model, where we think of a provider in financial terms, he was a failure.'

As long as women carry and breastfeed children, gendered roles will still be part of hetero relationships, and even same-sex couples having children find that childcare, at least at the start, can fall to one of the parents. But it's not just having children that affects who is bringing the money in either: illness, redundancy, the ups and downs of modern careers, all mean there might be times when one of you is providing money for two of you. But that doesn't mean it's easy to work through. We still attach a lot of our worth to the amount of money we earn, and the pressures of ego, shame and resentment can unravel otherwise healthy relationships.

'I became someone who couldn't do anything right.' Darlia, 32, is 'working things through' with her boyfriend after nearly breaking up with him following a tumultuous year that followed being made redundant. 'After losing my job I floundered. I just closed my eyes to money problems and spent on my credit card. Which wasn't great but it was also not the worst thing in the world; it's manageable. But once my boyfriend knew, he saw me as failing in everything: who I was hanging out with, what I ate, my weight. But he never had a problem with those things when I was earning good money.'

Our attitudes to money can often blind us. Many things might be playing out in Darlia's relationship; a lack of money might prompt fear in her partner, which comes out as aggression. It sounds like he really wants to be able to say, 'Your debt really scares me and I'm annoyed that you have got us both into this situation', but because he isn't comfortable discussing money, he chooses to take aim at what he sees as easier subjects: her weight, her diet, her friends.

Different attitudes towards money can be hard to talk around, because they're so loaded with emotion, but Eric Dammann has some calming words: 'A thing to realise, bar the real extremes – a shopaholic or a true gambling addict – there is not a right way to be with money; there are many ways to be with money, and they are all OK within reason. So when you get a spender and a saver and they get together, one of the key things for each to understand is that there are many ways to be with money. They are not right or wrong; the point isn't to make the spender a saver and the saver a spender.'

Jess, 26, moved in with her boyfriend last year. 'My boyfriend burns through money. He calls the ridiculous amount of trainers he has a "collection", which pisses me off – if I had that many shoes, it would just be known as "too many shoes".' Jess and her boyfriend are trying to save up to go travelling around South East Asia for six months. They both work in retail, earning about £23k a year. 'I'm constantly trying to get him to take saving for our trip seriously. I'll end up arguing with him because he bought expensive ice cream or Neal's Yard shower gel, when really that tenner isn't going to get us to Thailand but him learning to budget might. I hate that he makes me feel like a nag.'

Jess is trying to exercise some control because she feels like she has none. 'A practical way for a spender and a saver to work together is to set some money into a joint savings account – a minimum amount agreed by both people,' Eric says. 'Then assign money to each individual to do what they want with. The spender might spend theirs unthinkingly, but that's OK, and the saver might save theirs, and that's OK too.' Eric's solution sounds reasonable but pretty idealistic. But then Jess's boyfriend is going to have to choose whether he is up for compromising his current lifestyle for six months off travelling around South East Asia. And 'nagging' isn't the best route to get them there.

But how to talk? Well, the wrong way to do it is whichever way is causing problems for your relationship. Evidently, with Jess feeling like she's 'nagging', they need an alternate approach. I ask Simonne what advice she would give a couple to start talking about a subject they may have avoided even with themselves. 'Maybe you can start with deeper questions that don't necessarily relate to your current money situation: "How do you feel about money?" "What drives your attitude towards money?" These conversations are important when there is a hang-up or an emotional block. They might never be needed if everything is fine, if you're earning as much as you need, if you're saving for the future, and both people are happy with the arrangement – maybe you never need to discuss what you learned in childhood and how your attitude towards money is influenced. But if there is a block or somebody is lying or closed then those questions become really important.'

There is no golden rule that works for every couple. If it works for both people in the relationship then you're doing the right thing. George, 42, and Freddie, 36, have been together for three years. George moved into a flat Freddie already owned. George earns £50k as a public servant and Freddie earns £34k as a social worker. George pays Freddie some money towards the mortgage which he sees as rent and puts a hefty amount into his own savings each month. George says, 'Freddie has a flat. I don't have any real financial security, so I'm saving so I'll have enough in the bank to know I'll never stay with Freddie for any other reason than I want to be with him. So many of my friends stay in relationships because they're too scared to split their assets or stand on their own feet financially.'

I asked George how he felt. 'My last relationship was a messy break-up, and he got quite bitter about money, but with Freddie money just doesn't get in the way. We've only been together three years, maybe we'll check in every few years and see if we're still happy with it.'

There are many ways to make it work: one person might pay 100 per cent, or you can militantly split everything down the middle, as long as both people feel respected and neither is being controlled by money. That's not to say it's easy. What you are looking for is some financial harmony, rather than an exact balancing act of percentages. A relationship should balance financial disparity and life's general turbulence to create equality. My boyfriend and I have a child but still don't have a joint account. We do check in on how we're both doing with money at least every two weeks, as we're freelance and our incomes are sporadic. We both religiously pay half the mortgage and would expect the other one to flag if we ever thought we couldn't. Our money is our own, but we work towards plans like buying a car together. Oh and we give each other cash gifts for birthdays and special occasions like Mother's Day … a bit strange, wouldn't work for everyone, but it works for us.

How to split the bills by what you earn

Say you earn different amounts yet both want to contribute the same percentage of your earnings towards the shared rent and bills. Here's a simple formula my statistician dad gave to me:

Wage A + Wage B = Wage AB
Rent ÷ Wage AB x Wage A = amount Person A should pay
Rent ÷ Wage AB x Wage B = amount Person B should pay

So for instance, if rent is £1,200 between the two of you, and person A earns £100k and person B earns £50k, then person A would pay £800 and person B would pay £400:

Person A: £1,200 ÷ £150k x £100k = £800
Person B: £1,200 ÷ £150k x £50k = £400

How to talk to your partner about money

Talk about it when there isn't an urgent issue – if you only ever talk about money when a bill arrives, then it's always going to be a pressured conversation. Before you talk about figures and start doing sums, make sure you have talked about the emotions of money. How anxious does it make you feel? Why do you find it difficult to talk about?

- Try chatting about what money means to you, what it meant to you growing up and what it meant to your parents.

- Hear your partner out. Listen more than you talk.

- Then you can start to talk about the direct issues affecting you: the unpaid council tax bill, whether you can afford to move flats or how to clear a credit card bill that is racking up interest.

- This isn't just one conversation. Check in regularly with each other. In fact, this is really important – one conversation is not going to solve everything; you need to make talking about money a casual thing, and only regularity will do that.

- When either of you have done something well – like set up a standing order or stuck to that week's budget – say it out loud and congratulate each other. We're simple beings and praise always works.

How to tell your partner about your debt

This is for people who might have lied or concealed debt from their partner. I know someone who only told their boyfriend of seven years about their debt after they were rejected for a joint mortgage and another who has been hiding red letters and has jeopardised their partner's credit rating because the debt is registered to a flat they share.

- So you've got some debt? Most people do. But as with anything in a relationship, it's important to be honest about it. Maybe let your partner know you have something to discuss in advance, so they can prepare. But don't set up the conversation like you're about to tell them someone has died. It's not the biggest deal in the world.

- Don't go to the effort and stress of having the conversation only to tell them a part truth. It's tempting to only reveal so much or to change the number slightly. If you do this it means you'll have to keep up with your own lie, and you won't get the relief of having come clean. That relief, that's what you want from this conversation.

- Have all the information ready: how much you owe and to whom. Your partner is probably going to want to know why you got into debt in the first place, the exact figure and when and how you plan to pay the debt off.

- In *The Communication Book*, Mikael Krogerus and Roman Tschäppeler advise to 'say enough to be understood, but don't say too much. Tell the truth, don't speculate, don't dupe the person into believing something different. Don't say anything irrelevant and don't change the subject.'

- Have a look into the help you can get before the conversation. There are many charities and organisations whose only purpose is to help people out with debt, no matter how big or small. StepChange is a brilliant place to start. There's more information in the debt chapter of this book.

- Lay out all the information, then listen to their reaction. Let them react. Remember they might find this stressful too, so however they react, try to stay calm.

- People get into and out of debt all the time. What might seem impossible can definitely be done (and if it does seem impossible, then it's even more important to talk to someone – whether your partner or an organisation that can help). Keep positive about your future. It's just debt and a bit of a lifestyle change. You can do it.

16

Breaking up

A break-up isn't just saying goodbye to a person. It's the ending of everything shared, all things you built together. It's the pulling apart of one entity into two. If a relationship is sharing pizzas, sofas, dogs and cars, then a break-up is the separation of crockery, the reluctant returning of a T-shirt. It's having no one to share a hotel room and its bill with, it's downsizing, it's remortgaging, it's no longer being able to afford to go to your friend's wedding, it's paying all the council tax, it's having nowhere to put your toothbrush because they took the holder.

To talk about the reality of break-ups we must acknowledge that a relationship is a lifestyle. Every relationship has its own economic ecosystem, and often the heartbreak that a split causes isn't just from losing the other person – it's from the lifestyle change.

'At 38 I ended up back at my parents' [house]. That sucked.' It's rare to see someone walk out of a relationship and into a better financial situation. While Sarah was with her girlfriend she hadn't considered what might happen if they broke up. That's how she ended up back living with her parents at 38 – she had no savings, there was no escape fund. They were renting a one-bedroom flat together, 'a cute flat, filled with light; there was no way I could afford to rent it on my own'. It's a familiar scenario. There's a growing demographic of people who can only afford to live with other people but who don't want to live with other people; Sarah chose her parents' house as 'the lesser evil, over flatmates found on the Internet'. If you're financially dependent on your partner, if you provide the support to someone else's busy career, then where are you left if your relationship breaks down?

Sometimes it's hard to fathom what life will be like outside of the four walls of a relationship. It's something we saw with the baby boomer generation; for them being single was such a shameful thing to be as an adult. It meant something had gone wrong. The emotional turmoil of separating is often coupled with the physical downsizing of homes, making a divorce very visual and very public. They're also expensive. Relocating after a divorce costs the average person £5,089, and the legal fees average out at £8,926 each. 'Chances are life as a single person versus life as a married person means you're going to be worse off financially and have less security,' financial therapist Simonne says, 'even in situations where you love each other and want the best for each other. The emotions can still rise to the surface around [the question] "What does fair mean now that we don't want to be together?"'

'In my experience, when someone is hurt sharing does becomes difficult,' Melissa, a divorce lawyer working in the UK, says. 'It's never going to be easy splitting one household into two. If you have enough money to achieve that then great, but the hardest cases are quite often those with much smaller amounts of money to divide. In those circumstances quite often someone is going to feel as though they have been left in a difficult financial situation, perhaps because the other person has more responsibility for the children and the children's needs will always take priority.'

Ridiculously, because I've never been divorced and only hear of divorce lawyers in cases like Paul McCartney splitting from Heather Mills, I had always pictured divorce lawyers getting involved when there were many assets to split, 'who gets the speed boat?' kind of thing. But of course the law also helps us normal people split less. 'When 50 per cent of the pot is not going to meet someone's needs that is when it can get difficult and undoubtedly stressful,' Melissa continues. 'Understandably they are probably fighting harder because they feel they have more to lose.'

At least if you're married there is a legal path to separating things 'fairly', even if it sometimes doesn't feel like that. But if you don't marry and one of you prioritises the other's career while being more of the homemaker, then you have no right to their pension. If you move in with someone and they already own a property, you have no financial rights. As Dan, a 35-year-old coming out of an eight-year relationship, found out: 'When I met Kerry she was buying a flat. I even hired a van to help her move in. After a year I moved in with her and paid half of the mortgage. I paid for fitted wardrobes and towards a new bathroom. But when we split, the "friendly" break-up became acrimonious the moment money was mentioned, and I realised Kerry had no plans to release any money for me for what I had put into the flat.'

Cohabitees have almost no legal claim to property. It's

horrible to think, but falling out of love might just be the worst financial decision you ever make.

'I didn't want to look grabby at all, so I took nothing. It didn't make me a better person though. No one thought that.' Charlie is still bitter about walking away from her eight-year relationship and not taking what was hers: her car, all of her furniture, some money from the house. 'I really cared what other people thought of me. But now I realise that no one was thinking, "At least she left him her car."' It's taken some time for Charlie to realise that she didn't need to punish herself financially because she felt guilt for ending the relationship. We use money to ease our conscience all the time – buying free-range eggs or giving a few pounds to a homeless person – so it's no surprise that we use money in the same way to negate break-up guilt.

I asked Melissa if this was common, if in her practice she saw people use money to offset guilt or bad behaviour? 'I have had a handful of cases where, for example, one party has been unfaithful and the affair has caused the marriage to break down. I have been instructed to perhaps make more generous financial proposals by way of compensating the other person for causing the breakdown of the relationship. If someone asks for my advice as to whether that is appropriate, I have to be honest and say that a court will not want to divide finances in such a way to compensate/punish parties for adultery. And as time moves on and financial realities set in, they may later regret offering too much in a first flush of guilt.'

What is the right way to break up with someone who

earns a lot less than you do? When you're in a relationship the person with more money often sets the standard of living for both people. 'You take them along for the ride. They have to live your life,' Conor, 38, says. Conor is rich; he has one of those beautiful four-storey Edwardian houses in Camberwell, London. He's very aware that the women he dates often assimilate to his life rather than he to theirs. It makes sense; he has a large, empty house, the money to take them on holiday and a fun social circle. 'You suck them into your life and that puts a pressure on the relationship. If it fucks up they're thrown back into their old life, yet I get to carry on living as I always have. How do I make a break-up fair?'

It's a difficult question. I understand Conor's dilemma: he doesn't owe his ex-girlfriend anything. They didn't marry and were together just under two years, but ultimately she risked more to be in the relationship than he did. When their relationship got serious she moved out of her rented flat and into his house. When they split she had to find a deposit and two months' rent on her modest salary. 'I gave her some money; £3k I think,' Conor tells me. 'Which felt weird, because it wasn't that I was paying her off or anything, but she had left her flatshare to move in with me and I wanted her to have a deposit to rent a flat. Is that weird?'

There is no denying that relationships are somehow based on our means – how many times have you seen someone move in with their other half to save money on rent? Or because something outside of their control pushes the move sooner, like a landlord hiking up the rent or a flatmate vacating a room? I don't find Conor's behaviour weird; he had the control, which creates an unfair balance. It's not that he has to pay off his ex-girlfriend out of guilt for ending the relationship, but acknowledging that his life carries on seamlessly while she has to move home feels right. And yes, she might not have paid him 'rent' when living in his house, but that was because they were trying to build a relationship together. She could have been saving a 'nest egg' or 'escape fund', but both would have meant mentally keeping one foot out of the relationship.

Obviously it was easy for Conor to give his ex that money, both emotionally (it eased his guilt) and financially. It's hard to remain true to financial promises made in a relationship, especially when you're feeling hurt or processing other promises that have been broken. Brett, who we met in the dating chapter, told me about the breakdown of one of his long-term relationships: 'Money became an issue with Douglas because he suddenly had none. After we broke up he moaned to our friends that I had never paid as much rent as he had, and I remember thinking that was very unfair, to go back on what we had agreed as a couple when we were together – that I'd pay less rent because at the time I earned less money – and use it against me in the break-up.'

Getting emotionally ready to stand on your own two feet after a relationship ends is often as necessary as coming to terms with the other person not being in your life. A break-up can mean having to have a conversation about money, a subject which you might have avoided your whole life. I've met people who have remained separated for years instead of divorcing, out of fear of having that conversation about money. Or they stay together because the idea of dividing everything feels too torturous. Melissa, the divorce lawyer, explains the most difficult part of the separating process: 'There are situations where parties just can't agree anything, including what belongs to who, and who should get what. If a dispute cannot be resolved by agreement, in my experience it is usually because the parties have completely different expectations as to what the other person might need to start their life over again once the separation process has concluded. One of the main factors when considering how best to divide matrimonial assets is what each party needs. Sometimes they'll have identical needs, sometimes you have two people with very different needs – perhaps one has more responsibility for the children and has a much lower earning capacity than the other. People can have very different views as to what is reasonable in terms of expenditure – how much do you need to buy a new home? How much should you spend on food shopping each week? When a couple commence divorce proceedings, we have a process that enables us to consider the parties' financial circumstances. Part of the process involves them preparing a schedule of expenditure. That helps us assess whether one party is going to have to pay the other person ongoing financial support to meet their essential needs. Some people do inflate what they think are reasonable needs. Perhaps it's what they have become used to during the marriage or maybe the people they mix with think it is reasonable and essential to have an allowance of £400 per month for their hair.'

There is no denying that your financial solvency affects whether two people even choose to separate. My two major break-ups both happened right after I was given a pay rise. I didn't plan them that way, at least not consciously, and at the time I refused to even consider whether the extra money played any role. But both break-ups were my doing, my choice. When one of my exes, in a conversation charged with bitterness, accused me of waiting for a promotion to break up with him, I was aghast with rage. The kind of indignant rage that only really comes with being caught out. I didn't want to admit, even to myself, that money was part of any of my reasons for ending the relationship. But in retrospect I have to admit that the money put wind in my sails (for want of a better expression). Money brings mobility and freedom, and I guess I suddenly didn't *need* the relationships as much. It helped with the uncertainty and fear of going it alone.

A break-up isn't just the moment you separate; it's also the process that partly defines the next stage of your life. It's not just no longer being with that person, it's no longer sleeping in that bed or that house or even that neighbourhood. Breaking up is as much about sharing as a relationship is, just with very different emotions driving the process. It's hard for us to envision the possibility of a break-up while we're in the process of planning for a life together, but perhaps, like knowing where the exits are, everyone should at least have an idea of whether their life jacket fits, just in case they have to jump ship.

LET'S TALK MONEY AND WORK

Where does your money come from? For most of us, it's from working. It's impossible for me to say we need to talk about money without going deep on how we earn it.

But we don't just work for money, which complicates the conversation. We work for love, for passion, for status, because we fancy our co-worker or like the view from our office. We work because it makes us feel good, because it validates our existence and because so many of us are addicted to it. But ultimately we work because we all need money for the roofs over our heads, the travel cards in our pockets and the pasta in our bellies. Even if you're one of those people who find it hard to draw a line between what is work and what is fun, you'll still know the bits you need to do to earn the money you need to survive. And that is what we're going to discuss here: is your relationship with how you earn money healthy? Are you earning the most you could be for the work you're already doing? Is freelance really freeing? Is your workplace paying you and other employees fairly? Are you being discriminated against in any way?

And, importantly, what does earning money cost us? Because the pursuit of money always costs something.

17

Talking to colleagues about what you earn

Asking someone 'What do you earn?' is up there as one of the most un-British things you can do. It's the kind of question you were told off for as a child when your curiosity outweighed your manners. But manners and politeness have been protecting a shit-heap of lies, inequality and in some cases outright illegal discrimination. Saying we shouldn't talk about money is affecting more victims than salary-show-offs. And indeed the 2018 pay audit – where British companies with more than 250 employees had to report their gender pay gap – proved that transparency really is key to greater equality.

The results revealed what we all suspected, that men are paid more than women, with eight out of ten companies reporting a gender pay gap. While the numbers didn't measure whether those undertaking equal work were being paid equally, they did reveal inequalities at every level – only 22 per cent of the top quartile of Google UK is women, while only 29 per cent of partners at the UK's largest law firms are women. Ryanair revealed a shocking 72 per cent pay gap, which exists because their pilots are typically men, whereas the comparatively poorly paid cabin crew are more likely to be women.

We now know that there isn't an industry that isn't underpaying women, from construction to the civil service to fashion. Equally, other pay gaps exist across all industries, whether based on class, race or disability. In 2017 the Equality and Human Rights Commission (EHRC) found the pay gap between disabled and non-disabled workers who do the same job to be 13.6 per cent. When looking at race wage gaps in the UK, there is a frustrating lack of reports and stats. In the US we know that for every dollar a white man earns, a white woman earns 80 cents, a black man earns 70 cents and a black woman earns 60 cents – a startling difference in earnings, that highlights the intersection of race and gender in inequality. In 2017, a report from the EHRC found that in the UK there has been very little narrowing of ethnic pay gaps since 1993, and for some groups they have actually increased, particularly amongst men. But useful like-for-like pay audits don't expose the worst of inequalities, where disability, race and gender intersect. The EHRC found that disabled men from the Bangladeshi community experience a pay gap of a staggering 56 per cent (compared with non-disabled, white, British men). None of this makes for comfortable conversation, but politeness isn't going to create change.

These sorts of statistics are useful because they allow us to discuss injustices in our society using numbers, and also because they provide evidence that backs up many people's lived experience. It was the 2018 pay gap audit that helped me come to terms with sexism I'd experienced at work. It was the type of discrimination that hummed away just below the surface, just a little too subtle for me to call it out. For the first ten years of my working life in advertising I felt like I was working in a boys' club: a feeling of being an outsider, of not being entirely welcome while still being expected to perform. Not quite Peggy from *Mad Men* but not far off. Individually, my male bosses and colleagues behaved well towards me, but they seemed to share this sense of entitlement, of belonging and being valued, that eluded me. The day the gender pay gap figures were released I logged on to the government website to review the places I'd previously worked. I found out that the gap at the first advertising agency I ever worked at, DDB, was 38.1 per cent. I can only imagine what the gap was ten years ago when I was employed there. Seeing those figures in black and white made me realise that I hadn't imagined what I sensed at the time: the men at DDB were valued 38.1 per cent more than me. No wonder I felt the divide.

You would think that the release of those figures would have made me angry. Instead I felt validated. The transparency was truly helpful. I finally felt I wasn't being lied to, and knew my experience wasn't something I had made up. We need to acknowledge and assess more wage gaps than just the gender gap. Everyone who has faced discrimination or suspects ingrained disparity in their workplace should have access to the numbers.

The two times I have learned about a personal pay gap, they were either exposed by force (the government audit) or by accident (the wages left on the notepad in the meeting room and then circulated around my place of work). This information shouldn't have to be forced into the open. A spirit of transparency would absolutely make workplaces better. For a start, prejudice would have fewer places to hide, and pay disparities wouldn't have the chance to develop.

While companies continue to hide salaries, we can take matters into our own hands. Until a couple of years ago many of us weren't allowed to talk about our salaries or ask our work colleagues about theirs – many companies' employment contracts forbade such a discussion. Not only was it considered impolite, it was against 'the law'. You couldn't casually ask your line manager how much they were paid, or even tell someone at work what you were earning. That companies held us accountable to this shows that they were afraid of the consequences of workers discussing salaries. Not being allowed to cross-reference our salary with our co-workers meant that the power stayed with the employer, and it meant employees didn't know their worth. If we start by talking to each other, then we can take back some of that power, and use our knowledge to our advantage.

Thankfully it's now illegal in the UK for companies to prohibit you from discussing your salary with co-workers. But just because we can, it doesn't mean we do. Erica Baker's experience is a case in point. In 2015, Baker, then a Google engineer in the US, made a spreadsheet with her co-workers that listed their salaries. She then shared it on Google's internal social network, and more and more Google employees started adding their salary data. The spreadsheet highlighted Google's inconsistency in pay determination, and led to discussions about gender and ethnicity pay gaps. Google disapproved of the salary spreadsheet, and Baker left the company soon after creating it. As the *Wall Street Journal* reported, 'Google wants everyone to be able to search for anything online – unless it involves the salaries it pays to its workers.'

Most of you are probably reading this thinking, 'Yeah, I'd

love to know what everybody else earns, but I don't want to tell anyone my salary.' No one wants to be the sacrificial lamb; salary still feels so personal and talking about it still feels like an experiment. That's what was so powerful about Erica Baker's spreadsheet: she found a way to allow everyone to share their salary at the same time. And she framed it as exposing Google and pay disparity rather than pitting individual employees against one another in terms of remuneration.

Sharing your salary doesn't mean broadcasting it across a crowd. 'I have a best friend who works in the same industry,' Gavin, 34, who works in PR, tells me. 'We have always shared our salaries with each other, and even that data point of one helps me gauge if I'm on track. It's very reassuring.' A small inner circle or, like Gavin, just one friend can be the support and conversation you need to make more informed choices.

'When I was made MD of a fifty-person business in 2014, one of the first things I was given was a list of everyone in the company and their salaries. I was shocked by how much the wages varied in the same department,' Katie, who runs a hardware development company, tells me. 'I knew as a company we were safe though because no one was going to discuss their wage with anyone in the building. There was one department of three where a man was earning £100k and two women were earning £30k. They were working under him, yet that salary disparity was huge. Obviously now that would be a situation I'd examine closely, but back then, even just a few years ago, I didn't question it through the lens of the gender pay gap.'

I hope the pay gap audit inspired many employers to truly look at inequalities in their team. I like to think that on that Thursday morning, when the stats were published, managers up and down the country had a dawning moment of realisation.

I spoke to someone who wanted to remain anonymous; she works for an investment bank that reported a 35 per cent pay gap in favour of men. She wanted to know whether she was actually being underpaid in comparison to her male colleagues who did the same job. When a friend whom she had a pretty good relationship with resigned from the business she asked him, 'I really want to know what you were being paid, because I need to know whether I am being paid correctly.' He was very open with her and happily their salaries were comparative. She admitted that resentment – an effect of the pay gap news – was building up within her, and that if she hadn't asked that personal question she would have felt underpaid, without ever knowing if it was true. It makes me think that every woman who works for a company that reported a significant gender pay gap must have felt victimised to some degree – yet the pay gap can't be affecting all of them equally.

The conversation between the two investment bankers illustrates the benefit of getting the so-called 'privileged' to talk. Talking about our own salaries means thinking about others, and recognising our place within a system. Racism, sexism, homophobia and classism all intersect with how much we are paid – who has it, who gets it and how much. Just as it shouldn't only be up to people of colour to call out racism, or for women to call out sexism, it shouldn't only be up to those who feel underpaid to call out financial privilege. That is not to say it's easy to own up to privilege, but ultimately admitting a privilege is like calling out a prejudice: it shows an awareness of the systems around us. We need to accept that recognising our privilege, or having it called out by others, is not a negative judgement on us as individuals, but an important recognition of the society we live in. Because the alternative is bleak: if we don't talk about privilege we just protect the idea that everything is fair and meritocracy is working.

There are many people in power who do not want their employees to casually discuss salaries. 'Creating tension', 'making the environment toxic and competitive', 'demoralising for some people', 'it can create jealousies' – these are the reasons I've been given by bosses for why we shouldn't discuss our salaries with our co-workers, though I can only see these as reasons employers shouldn't pay their staff unfairly.

I know it feels shameful and uncomfortable to talk about pay with colleagues, and I'm not saying you need to be like Baker and tell everyone – but know that as long as you're not sharing with anyone, you're somewhat complicit in creating an environment where your employer may benefit to the detriment of you and your colleagues. As David Burkus writes in his book *Make Salaries Transparent*, 'secrecy leads to what economists call "information asymmetry", a situation in which one party in a negotiation has more or more accurate information than the other party has. Although both sides of a salary negotiation have access to privileged information (both the employer and the prospective employee know her old salary), the employer holds a much greater amount of privileged information (the salary of everyone in the company and the budget for the position) and is therefore able to gain an advantage in most situations.'

Transparency between colleagues is one way to address

OPEN UP

this 'information asymmetry'. Another way is through altering the balance of power. In 2016, the American state of Massachusetts did just that. They barred employers from asking applicants their salaries before offering them a job. The law requires hiring managers to state a figure upfront based on what an applicant is worth to the company, rather than just bettering what they made in a previous position. The law was put in place in an attempt to make sure a discriminatory pay gap doesn't follow people from job to job.

Think about this: how many of your colleagues already know your salary? If you work for a company or an organisation the answer is probably more than you think: your manager and their manager will know; the finance department all know; IT probably have access to the payables spreadsheet; all of HR will know; the MD, the CFO and the CEO definitely know; and then throw in a couple of people who might have been privy to conversations about you or your team. It's really not a secret. So why are you hiding it? Awkwardness probably. You might be embarrassed that you earn more than some and don't want to risk losing that advantage. You might be a minority and feel vulnerable. You might not want to know how much less you're paid because you fear your own anger. You might believe that ignorance is bliss.

I understand that everyone comes to this with different experiences and different levels of power.

Freelancers are definitely better at sharing. There seem to be two main reasons for this. One, they negotiate money all the time, so sharing can have an immediate effect. Two, a rate for a job isn't their entire salary, which means they're not fully revealing their income and putting themselves up for complete scrutiny.

On 12 May 2018 the freelance journalist Richard Godwin wrote a piece for the *Guardian* entitled 'How Much Do You earn?' In the piece he revealed his own (private sector, freelance) salary. It was the first piece of its kind, in a mainstream publication, where the journalist (or presenter) discussing greater transparency outed themselves, and what a relief it was. Richard took the decision to reveal his whole yearly earnings, writing, 'My gross income was £70,242 on my last tax return, which would put me in the top 5 per cent of British earners. I find that at once reassuring and awkward. Once I lopped off expenses, my income was £49,250.' Even in an article about salaries it felt like a ballsy thing to commit to print. While reading the piece I wondered if Richard Godwin's fingers had hovered over his keypad for a moment before he punched in all five figures ...

'As soon as I was commissioned, I knew there were no two ways around this. It would be hugely cowardly to go around asking people to reveal their wages and not reveal mine. I felt it had to go with the territory. I was very nervous about it,' Richard told me when I followed up to find out what the reaction had been to him revealing his salary. Had his world imploded? Was he now hiding in shame? Were his friends still speaking to him? 'I did think, Oh my goodness, when people read this, am I going to be taken down for my privilege? Are people going to say, "You have it easy because you are white and male"? You fear that kind of judgement. Especially with the *Guardian* and the commentators. I found that actually in revealing it no one can really accuse you of anything. Because it's just a number. I realised that once the number is out there you're less anxious about it.'

Richard pointed out another very interesting issue with

keeping our salaries secret: 'I think it [the shame and secrecy that surrounds our salaries] makes you suspicious of your own success, and stops you taking a legitimate pride in it. I have worked really quite hard for diminishing pay and worse conditions. Just to survive as a freelance journalist is a mild achievement. If you'd have told me at 16 I would be writing articles for the *Guardian* I'd have been like, "Wow that is amazing." And all this suspicion around pay takes away some of the pleasure from our own achievements.'

I wondered whether people who worked for companies with completely transparent pay policies felt differently about the money hitting their account each month. Were they more positive than those encouraged to hide their salaries? I arranged a call with Hailley, a PR specialist who works for the tech company Buffer (an app that schedules tweets and Facebook posts for you). I knew Hailley's salary before I spoke to her; a quick Google search and there it was on a spreadsheet: $90,091. Not only does Buffer have a completely transparent pay policy, but their method of working out each employee's pay is transparent too, and is done by a set formula. Hailley tells me, 'it means we talk openly about money with each other. For instance a colleague was helping me work out how to file my tax, and to do so, he just pulled up his tax forms, where I could see every number, and he took me through the process. Another colleague has shared the amount of her mortgage and how [she] and her husband manage it. We are just so open about all things money, which means I've learned a lot about managing my personal finances while working at Buffer.'

And the transparency around money doesn't stop with Hailley's colleagues. 'I am much more open with friends now, and it adds so much to my conversations, especially around life choices – moving jobs, buying a house. Someone's financial situation is a whole additional layer that I didn't know before, and that adds a lot of clarity to understanding what someone's perspective on a situation might be.' But Hailley also tells me about friends of hers who refuse to ever look at her salary; even though they know it's available in a couple clicks on Google, they don't want to betray that friendship code. 'I think they feel if they know mine, they'll have to reveal theirs. My salary has actually gone down since I started working at Buffer. Which is interesting to talk about. In the salary formula at Buffer, location affects the amount you are paid; I moved from San Francisco to Toronto, where the cost of living is more reasonable, so my salary went down by $20k. When it went down, it brought up a lot of emotions for me. Sort of like, "Do I not contribute enough?", "How is this reflecting my value to the company?" But that is why the formula is so helpful, because I could see the added $20k was for being able to live in San Francisco. It had nothing to do with my worth. I discussed how I felt with colleagues, which helped, and I actually now feel positive about it decreasing, because I managed to separate my worth from the number that is assigned to me.'

As a method for equality, transparency is working: there is no pay gap at Buffer between men and women who do the same job. I asked Hailley how it might affect her future career choices and whether she would like to work for a place that doesn't publish her salary online. She says, 'there is a lot of trust that comes from this level of transparency. I very much trust my manager, I trust the leadership at Buffer, I trust my colleagues. This added level of not just salary transparency but the "why" behind your salary too [that comes from the set formula Buffer uses to work out all employer salaries]. It's now baked into me, and it would be very difficult to go anywhere which didn't have a certain level of transparency.'

Transparency is where we're heading, I'm certain of it. Sharing empowers ourselves and others. The better we get at discussing our salaries, the more confident we'll be when it matters – when we negotiate our own.

18

Getting paid what you are worth

So many of the articles in print at the moment on 'Asking for a Pay Rise' or 'Negotiating your Salary' fail to address that there are two humans in the room, not just an employee and their robotic boss. So here are some humans who have been employees, and are now bosses. The best advice I've received on how to ask for more has always been from people who have been on both sides of pay negotiations. So I spoke to some of the top senior people at brands I love and respect and asked their advice on how to get ahead in work. I prodded and pried into how they feel about money conversations and what it's like giving a pay rise – or having to say no. More money may not be the key to happiness, but everyone should be fairly compensated for their work, and the first step to that is feeling comfortable talking about your salary with the person who pays you.

Meet Pip Jamieson

Pip started her career in marketing, working for MTV in Australia and New Zealand. In 2009, she swapped marketing for matchmaking, founding The Loop, a more creative version of LinkedIn. In 2014, Pip founded her current venture, The Dots, a platform that connects creatives and freelancers with commercial opportunities.

Pip on overestimating your salary

Personally I feel really comfortable talking about pay. I see the most important part of my role is to attract and retain world-class talent, and pay is fundamental to that. I have amazing people, and they deserve to be paid what they are worth, but such a big part of my role is making sure I am paying them correctly and not under- or overpaying them.

Tech salaries are pretty punchy these days, and I have seen it become a detriment when people go in above their odds. The challenge is when someone goes too punchy or too senior for their level. You are accountable for your performance; if you are not performing to the level of your pay grade then my other job as a CEO is to look at that and make sure that the company is efficient for the sake of all of my team. I have had to have those awkward conversations where I end up saying, 'I'm spending more on you than the output I'm getting.'

On being comfortable chatting money

For me personally I think conversations about money and pay are such an important part of what I do. I also never want anyone in my business to feel uncomfortable having these conversations. The worst thing that can happen to me is that I lose a rock star member of my team because they don't feel they are being paid their worth and I find out after they have left. Losing someone brilliant and trying to replace them is a nightmare, and costs the business a lot of money.

On honesty and transparency in pay reviews

If a boss says no to a pay rise request it is really important for a boss to explain why. A good leader shouldn't stop at a 'no'. A good leader should say, 'No, and this is why …' A no could be because the business is in trouble and can't financially support a pay rise right now. It could be because the person asking is not ready yet – but then an action plan should be put in place: 'If you do this, this and this by X, we can discuss a raise then.' Leaders should be more transparent in how a business is functioning.

On picking the right time to ask

Get your boss in a good mood. It can be so nerve-racking that sometimes you can be like, 'I've learned my script, I'm ready, I need to do it right now!', and the challenge is remembering that your boss is busy and they might be trying to deal with their own massive stresses right at that moment. People can forget the emotional side of things. If you grab your boss when they are stressed or running between meetings they are going to be less amenable. You don't want them to consult the priority list in their head and think, 'I can't deal with this right now.' So be empathetic and think, 'When is my boss in a good mood? When do they have time to talk this through?' Those emotional things really make a difference in terms of negotiating your pay rise. People are always more amenable to change when they are in a good mood.

On finding the right support network

I am in a number of female CEO groups where we are very candid with each other, and it is amazing having a support group where I am able to have open conversations and ask candid questions like, 'Is this normal?' or 'Is it just me or is this guy being a tool?'

So a team of peers to talk to is great, but I will caveat that by saying, be sure to surround yourself with people who challenge you. If people like you they will naturally be on your side, but sometimes if you are very upset about something, you don't want them to agree because they have empathy for you; you want them to say, 'Maybe you want to think about how you were in that situation.'

Meet Caroline Pay

Caroline has been one of the top creative directors in the UK for most of her career. She led creative agencies BBH and Grey before moving to LA to head up creative at Headspace.

Caroline on the power of surprise

I love talking about money. I love it. I love, love, love negotiating, and I think people don't expect women, creatives or British people to want to talk about it – the three reasons people are surprised when I am so up for talking about money. And I think taking people by surprise with courage and bravado is the best way to get a pay rise.

On striking while it's hot

One time I had a review. The person doing the review had all the emails where colleagues had reviewed me printed out, and he said, 'I've never had something so positive, this is amazing, it's resoundingly positive', and went on and on and on ... So I said, 'Great, let's talk about money', and he said, 'No, this isn't a pay review', and I was like, 'Hang on, you've just told me this is the best review you've ever seen, and you don't expect that to have any financial value? This is what I expect following this review, and if you don't expect to deliver that, then show me a review where you would.' I asked for the rise to be sorted 'by this time tomorrow'. And it was.

On weak bosses

I hate reactive pay rises [when someone gets another job offer with the intention of using it to get a pay rise from their existing company]. That is the fucking bane of my life, and I think it's a sign of a weak boss and a weak relationship. My ideal is proactive pay-rising, and I like surprising people with a pay rise, rather than them having to ask for it.

Sometimes a friend at another agency is trying to steal a team [in advertising, creatives often work in teams of two where they are hired together and earn the same amount] from me and I'll call him up and say, 'Hey, you're about to give this team a 100 per cent pay rise and they're not worth it, so rather than stealing from me, call me up and let's chat about it, let's have that conversation.' Although sometimes people hire people from me and I'm like, 'Thanks very much, you've taken them off my hands.'

On getting people the right money

If someone is asking for a pay rise and you think they deserve it and you have the ability to go and argue and negotiate for it, it always works. If I think someone deserves a pay rise, I've never not got it for them.

But the most interesting bit for me is if someone asks for a pay rise and you don't think they deserve it – I have come up with a way of dealing with it. Let's say there's a team who get paid fine but they haven't had a pay rise in years and were hired before my time. So they come to me to ask for a pay rise. They're crying, they're angry, they say to me, 'We get paid £28k yet we've looked around the market and spoken to headhunters and we know we are worth £48k.' I have to say 'Number one we don't have any money, number two that's a ridiculous jump, and number three, if you look at the work you have done, it's not worth a massive pay rise. But what we are going to do is work out how we can get you to £48k. So let's say we'll get you to £35k in six months, then £40k in twelve months and in eighteen months' time you will be on £48k. But to get there you need to start delivering this kind of work.' So they go out super happy and super motivated, and in the end they get the money they want and I get an astonishing team. It works. It's happened – teams come back firing on all cylinders.

On asking gutsy questions

When I'm moving jobs and negotiating for myself, I always ask them, 'How can you make sure I come away from this conversation and feel that this is the best decision I've ever made?' Then the negotiation becomes interesting because we talk about things over and above money, and that's when the chat gets very human.

Bring everything to a pay rise conversation

What gets you a pay rise is changing the destiny of the agency, whether that is culturally, creative, doing panels or winning awards. So make sure you list everything you do for your job, even if it's not strictly on your list of responsibilities.

Meet Lydia Pang

Lydia describes herself as a 'Frankenstein creative'; her vast and varied portfolio spans concept creation, talent commissioning, creative leadership and visual strategy. Since 2016, Lydia has worked as the creative director of Refinery29, the leading global media company focused on young women.

Lydia on putting out the first number

My dad is a really strong businessman, and he has always said, 'Never say the first number, because the second you ask for a number, you are capping yourself at that number.' Get in there and state your case. Give the hard data and say, 'I have won this many pitches' or 'I brought in this much revenue.' Whenever I have done that, the number that my employers have come back with has been bigger than the number I was going to say. Like my dad says, 'No one will look someone in the eye and agree with all the things they have done and then lowball them.'

I've seen it from the other side. It will be July time, half-year review, and someone in my team will say to me, 'You know I feel like I am doing really well. I have led on a few projects and I did that big pitch and I am looking for $5k or $10k more', and I am thinking in my head, 'Well, that is interesting, I had a number for you, but now that you have said that number and I know you are going to be happy with that, I would rather just give you that because I need to save money.'

On not being too thankful

There was a time where I was very thankful when talking about money. I was all, 'Thank you for your mentorship and

177

your advice.' I think that works when you are a little younger, but when you get older I wouldn't advise on being that passive, and being all, 'Oh thank you so much for this £2k pay rise, I really appreciate it.' Now that I'm older, I very much know my worth – if I don't get it here, I will go somewhere else – and I like to bring that confidence into the room, even if I don't say those words.

On playing the game

I was talking to a girl in New York recently, she is a senior art director, desperate to be promoted, and she said to me, 'Oh I never lie. I never lie about the amount of money I have made in the past', and I was like, 'What do you mean?' She was like, 'Well, if I go to another job, they say, "How much money were you on?" I say the amount.' When I heard that, a part of me was conflicted, and I did think, 'Wow, amazing to be so honest', but at the same time I was like, 'Everyone else is lying, so maybe lie?!'

On learning from the Americans

In the UK we are apologetic, self-deprecating, modest. We like people to come up to us and crown us with a promotion. But in America people ask for one. They are like, 'Oh I am going to let you know that I am the best person in this room. I am also going to let you know that the idea that just surfaced across the room was mine – I'm going to stamp my name on that and let you know.' I sit in a lot of meetings and think, 'All these bitches stood up to their idea, claimed their idea and put their name on their idea and I didn't. I lost out here by not being a little more awake.'

Meet Katriona Fraser

The Talent Business is the world leader in talent for businesses fuelled by innovation and creativity. Kat has worked with them for twelve years. As well as working with companies and finding the right talent for the right job, part of Kat's role is working with people to find the right career path for them.

Katriona on thinking short-term first

A lot of people come to me and say they want to move jobs because they don't feel valued, or they want to make a big leap financially. I always say, 'You can move jobs, but you could also let your current employer know how you are feeling.' Moving jobs is a pretty drastic and permanent solution to something that could be solved with a conversation.

On doing your research

Go on Google, go and look at salary surveys, go and talk to peers, go and talk to headhunters, look at LinkedIn, ask a forum (they're often quite fruitful) – there are so many ways to find out what you should be being paid these days. Maybe there is somebody exiting your business that you are mates with that you can have a conversation with?

On working for just the money

I get increasingly more people coming to me and saying they're not as motivated by creative opportunities from their nine-to-five, because they can fulfil them outside of their day job with a side hustle, so their day job must pay well. Also people have different financial pressures on them … marriage breakdowns are happening more and more these days, and people are saying to me, 'I'd rather take the cash and do something that perhaps does not excite me as much.'

On asking for too much

When I'm negotiating someone's salary in a new job people sometimes say, 'I want £20k more', and I say, 'Don't do that. Go in, prove your worth and get that pay rise, because my god, that £20k will put so much more pressure on your shoulders.' I think I would rather be in the situation where I prove it and get rewarded for it. I do tell them to be very clear about setting those goals: put a date in the diary for when that review might be, and say, 'I will accept this salary now, but I would really love to have a salary conversation in six months' time, now that we have some very clear goals in mind.' Much better to do that than go in with a really punchy salary and have to fill those boots very quickly.

And when something goes tits up within a company, they are going to look at the bottom line and they are also going to look at the salaries they are paying and go, 'Right, who's the highest paid here?' If someone hasn't quite lived up to their expectations, then you are unfortunately the first to go. If you're paid too much you can find yourself in quite a vulnerable situation, I think.

On negotiating time and flexibility

I'm talking to Facebook at the moment; they are discussing a new model where they get the very best people to commit to them for, let's say, 50 per cent of the year, but those people can use that time up whenever they want. I think it is definitely the way more and more businesses are going, and it's a conversation that we are having more and more often.

On hearing 'no'

You read about this and people say this all the time: 'Go on, ask for a pay rise. The worst that can happen is they can say "no".' That's true, but actually hearing 'no' can be massively demoralising and demotivating. I think, whatever happens and even if they say 'no', you need to come out of that conversation knowing exactly what you need to do to achieve the pay rise, so that next time they say 'yes'.

Meet Michelle Kennedy

After training as a lawyer and working through the ranks at the dating networks Bumble and Badoo (reaching deputy CEO at the latter, a £100m+ company), Michelle Kennedy is now using her tech wisdom and passion for connecting people for her own venture, Peanut, a social network for mums.

Michelle on asking for a rise or promotion

Someone once told me to go in and advocate for yourself as you would a teammate. If you were talking about someone in your team, you would go in with all guns blazing, and you would say exactly why they deserve it, what they do and what they contributed, and yet when it comes to advocating for yourself, it feels awkward. It can feel like you are being formal, or it feels like you are asking for something that you are not entitled to. So battle for yourself as you would a friend.

On always being prepared to talk money

I was once sat next to a very successful entrepreneur at dinner.

She had just exited her own business, she had money to invest and she was asking me about Peanut, about raising and the valuation. She said to me, 'So talk to me about raising money, and talk to me about where you are and what you need', and I was like, 'Oh I don't want to talk about it over dinner', and I even said, 'I am not raising at the moment.' She paused, looked at me and said, 'Michelle, as an entrepreneur, you are always raising, and you are always willing to talk about it, regardless of where you are.'

On having a plan B

Before a friend or mentee goes in for a pay rise I always ask, 'What are you going to do if you don't get it? What's your plan B?' I think people should always know what they will do if the answer is no – ask yourself, 'Is it a deal-breaker for you? Will you move on? Will you give yourself six months to find somewhere else?' I think having a plan B will give you confidence, because then you can go in thinking, 'If I get it great, if I don't, it doesn't matter because I love what I do' or, 'If I get it great, and if I don't that's really it for me and I am going to move on.'

On earning top dollar

Leaving Badoo was one of the hardest decisions, and that was in no small part down to money – I was making amazing money, and my lifestyle was great accordingly. I stepped away to start my own thing and have had no salary for two years. I can't even remember what it is like to have a salary.

The potential of doing my own thing was really exciting for me, and I wanted to do it. I felt prepared and I also felt like if I don't do it now I will literally never do it.

From my role at Badoo, there would only be a handful of roles that I could potentially get in London, and I would be doing similar work to Badoo, running someone else's company – and I wanted to run my own. So that is the thing: being overpaid can lead to complacency and not wanting to move, because there are very few roles which would pay you as much. And I really believe it's only by pushing yourself to do something really uncomfortable that amazing things come.

Meet Dr Martino Picardo

Dr Picardo is an independent consultant and the former CEO of Stevenage BioScience Catalyst. He is also currently Entrepreneur in Residence (great title!) at the University of Manchester Technology Transfer Company.

Martino on the difficulty of negotiating when they already know what you earn

I applied for a CEO role, and that came with a salary. As I found out later, that salary happened to be at the lower end of the range for CEO jobs. I negotiated as well as I could, but of course they knew how much I was earning, so they could gauge how much more to give me. If they don't know your current salary you are in a much better position to negotiate.

On earning more than your employees

It's about responsibility and accountability. I was the one who had to go into a board meeting every three months and explain – sing for your supper, I call it – how the company is performing. As the CEO, you set the company objectives for the year, in agreement with the board. Those company objectives are your personal objectives as CEO – you carry the can, not the finance director or the business manager or the builder's assistant or the receptionist. That's why you earn the big bucks, so I have no guilt associated with that. What I tried to do was make sure that people working for me felt like they were earning an honest living. No one left because they weren't getting paid enough.

On different approaches

If I had to make a sweeping generalisation, I would say that women tend to avoid confrontation as much as possible. I've been managed by women as well, and they were generally better prepared to have the conversation early and in advance of an appraisal, rather than wait for the appraisal to tell you that you weren't going to get a pay rise. In my sector – and all I can really talk about is life sciences – I've noticed a big North/South divide. People tend to deal with not getting a pay rise much better in the North, maybe because there are less options for life sciences jobs in the North.

On giving a pay rise and the importance of formalising the process

For the last six or seven years, because of austerity, people just haven't been getting big pay rises. Depersonalising it is always the best way, because that conversation can be very difficult. The hard bit is looking someone in the eye and saying, 'Maybe you're not doing as well as you think you are.' The best appraisals are not just one-on-one; they include 360 feedback. In a bigger organisation, you're a line manager to one person and you're being appraised by someone else; you're part of a chain. So I ask for feedback from the team, from other managers (not just their manager), from the people they work with every day. People are looking for consistency, transparency and for the manager to articulate the 'why not'.

19

What is success exactly?

When I was nearly six months pregnant I pulled an all-nighter at work. No one made me, I chose to. I didn't think the work I'd produced was good enough, and there was a big presentation the next day. So I roped in a couple of members of my team, worked all night, got a cab home in the morning to pick up my passport and promptly flew to Geneva to present. Success, I had always presumed, was a struggle. If I wanted success I had to work for it. It had never occurred to me that true success was a good life, not a job title and a salary.

Too often, how we make money defines us. If there's a talking head on TV, we're given three pieces of information: Sue, 33, accountant. Many of our most common surnames come from trades: Mason, Smith, Taylor, Cook. Our job titles have been so tightly tied to our identity. Yet many of us don't, and don't want to, self-identify as a job title. It is a real problem within our culture that one of the first things people want to know about us is how we make money. When you're asked, 'What do you do?' you're expected to answer with what you do to make money. If you balance spreadsheets for a living but your hobby is making bread, you're not supposed to say 'bread-maker'. No, Sue – until you've commercialised it, you can't identify as it.

For so long society has hinged so much of our success and status on our job title and salary. We project on to work like we project on to money; it can be our definition of success, of status. But what can you really tell from a job title? 'Creative director' might sound interesting, creative, dynamic and very 'in charge', but the reality could be miniature Pret sandwiches in boardrooms located just outside the North Circular debating average typography. Equally an 'influencer', with a huge following and great clothes, might spend most of her time crying about the comments she receives from strangers about her parenting.

Brilliantly, we've started to decouple success from money and power, and reject that there is only one way to be successful. Arianna Huffington wrote a manifesto to redefine success 'beyond the two pillars of money and power' in her book *Thrive*. Tom Hodgkinson rallied for an antidote to a work-obsessed culture in his book *How to be Idle*, and Emma Gannon de-stigmatised the 'slashy' (those hopping around different jobs) by renaming them 'multi-hyphenates'.

These books are all pushing against a real problem. We've been sold success as a singular destination, that if you work hard enough you'll get there, and then you'll be happy. The problem with this 'dream' is that no one knows what a let-down money and status can be until they've dedicated years of their life working towards them. 'At school we are conditioned to be ambitious, go-getting and to achieve our potential,' Katie, who worked for Nike for many years, tells me. 'You do it because you're promised that the higher you climb the better life will be. But what I saw at the company I worked my ass off for in my twenties was that by 32 everyone had divided into two packs: those who wanted a better life, who realised that while on paper the job looked great, the day-to-day reality was toxic and pretty demoralising; and then there were those who were OK as long as it sounded really good at a New York cocktail party.'

I speak to so many people who have worked hard to reach a certain position or title only to get there and realise that it's, well, just another job title, not paradise. We're learning that success doesn't have to be a meteoric rise to the top in pursuit of a bigger salary, but if it isn't that, what does it look like? Freelance? Founder? Part-time florist? Stay-at-home dad?

The current conversation is redefining success as a work-life balance, but is it all positive? 'At the moment, a woman going freelance is the ultimate middle finger to the corporate career.' Brittany Bathgate, a successful fashion blogger with 220k Instagram followers, left her retail job with a steady salary to work for herself earlier this year. 'But adjusting to freelance has been hard. Some days I didn't even want to get out of bed. It's definitely not the answer for everyone.' A friend I often work with raises another very good point: 'If we're heroing people who choose a life balance, what does it mean in real terms? Say I told you I wasn't that bothered about getting to the top in my field – how would you as my work colleague feel about that? Would that colour your view of my ability to do my job?'

And of course, with any work, we all have salary expectations. We need to pay bills and rent. We have families to support, friends to drink with and weddings in Cornwall to get to. But we should always be mindful just how much money and status are figuring in our decision-making. If money and status are the two primary reasons you've accepted a job then you are probably not going to be happy in that job for long. If you find what you do morally reprehensible, if your colleagues annoy the hell out of you or you're just bored a lot of the time then you should question why you are doing it. You might have the job title, you might have the salary, but those things don't always result in a better life. As Tim Ferriss, author of *The 4-Hour Workweek*, says, 'if you ever find yourself saying, "But the money is good", then you're probably in the wrong job'.

There are numbers other than our salary that we judge our success by: followers and likes. Success on the Internet can feel similar to the success of landing a prestigious job: short-lived euphoria rather than contentment. I wonder if this is because they both depend on comparing favourably to others? I spoke to the world's first comparison coach, Lucy Sheridan, and asked her about the dangers of success as a comparative: 'In terms of how we define our own success, we should make sure we're looking at examples of other people as stimulus only. Not with, "That's *the* way to do it" but, "That's *a* way to do it – what does that mean for me?"' Lucy also warns of not being blinded by other people's success: 'Typically an overnight success is about three years working hard behind the scenes. People who come out with a successful product, book, launch, etc. – they work their arses off for ages and finally there's a tipping point, and suddenly the snowball takes itself down the mountain and you don't have to touch it. But on social media that success looks like it came about quickly.'

As Katherine Ormerod writes in her book *Why Social Media is Ruining Your Life*, 'while you might roll your eyes at hearing social media stars talk about their workload, it's worth remembering that if it were so easy to build a successful social media business, everyone would have quit their jobs and be running successful YouTube channels by now. Most social media mavens are workaholics, who don't really understand the meaning of downtime, and the competition is fierce.'

As a rule, whether online or off-, more money tends to mean more work and more stress. Elite men in the US work longer hours than poorer men in the US. It used to be thought that money allowed a life of leisure, but that's no longer the case. There is always a pay-off for more money (time, sanity, responsibility, autonomy). And when I asked 'rich' people how they felt about money, we saw that they didn't feel rich, they just wanted more, which begs the question: how much more of their time and sanity are they willing to give?

We fetishise work and working. We live in a very busy society. I'm 'busy', my friends are 'busy'; as Tom Hodgkinson wrote in *How to Be Free*, 'When people say "I just don't have enough time" they mean "I prioritised something else."' It's said that Apple CEO Tim Cook routinely begins emailing employees at 4.30 a.m. in the morning, and that the now former Yahoo CEO Marissa Mayer worked 130-hour weeks. If the successful and rich are just working more then are they really successful? Should we not assess what might be lost in life in the pursuit of money and 'success'?

Many of us find ourselves in an industry where because we've worked hard for our position, the industry's markers of success really begin to matter to us – after all it's what we are surrounded with all day. It's not to say being on an upward trajectory can't be motivating and rewarding, but it's easy, when we're amongst it, to be blinded by a very prescriptive version of success: getting to be a 'level two' at work or 'partner', or 'chartered' or 'published'.

There is a danger in allowing a job title or a salary to determine your identity. Zoe Cohen, an executive coach, told me about her own experience letting go of an identity. 'I was an NHS director. I had been a director for nine years, and it was a big part of my life. It was a big part of my identity too. I knew I wanted a career shift and a life shift, so I chose to leave the NHS to coach full-time, but I also knew how hard I would find leaving behind my identity as a "director". I had to coach myself through the transition to my new identity over a period of months.'

I know how Zoe felt. I used to work in advertising. I'd got to the top of the industry, as one of the few female executive creative directors. After going back to work following maternity leave I realised I no longer wanted to do that job. It wasn't making me happy like it once had; it was making me miserable, which meant I was making the people I loved miserable. But letting go of the job title and the corresponding salary was hard. 'People don't throw away jobs they've worked really hard for,' I thought. The surprising part was that I was unaffected by the lifestyle change from earning less. The part I found most difficult was losing the status of a 'six-figure earner'.

I realised I'd handed my happiness over to the opinion of a handful of ex-colleagues and strangers, and while trying to earn their respect, I was being crap to the people I loved – my partner, my son and my close friends. 'If we are ever in "should" mode, that is a big red flag, because it means that we're being influenced by things outside of ourselves,' says Lucy Sheridan. '"Should" means we've outsourced our power, our direction or our decisions, and we need to claw that back.'

Another reason it's important to know who you are without your job is because they don't last for ever. I've heard redundancy described as a form of identity theft. Its effect is big enough that the government has set up an initiative to provide therapy to people who have been made redundant. It's not just money worries and job security that causes the psychological crisis that can happen after redundancy; not feeling valued, not having a place to go every day, no longer having that camaraderie with colleagues and a loss of identity are all thought to have effects as great as the financial strain of losing a job. Liv Siddall started a warm, chatty podcast this year called *Redundancy Radio* after – you guessed it – being made redundant. I asked her how she chose the name. 'My dad kept saying to me at the time, "You are not 'redundant'. Just say that you left, don't tell anyone you were made redundant. Don't use that word", but by talking about it and owning it, it doesn't define me.'

Success is many things: to many people it's a blue tick, it's money, it's life balance, it's driving an Audi, it's owning redundancy. But true success is the freedom to make choices. Sheryl Sandberg gave us the term 'jungle gym' to replace the tired 'career ladder' in her book *Lean In*. 'There's only one way to get to the top of a ladder but there are many ways to get to the top of a jungle gym. Plus a jungle gym provides great views for many people not just those at the top.' Who says we shouldn't apply that thought to salary? The idea that salary should go up and up until we take our pension is not only exhausting but untenable – most of us will experience change in our working lives that will be reflected in our salaries, and that's OK. Wouldn't it be better to measure success by thinking of it as a path where the more accomplished we become, the more choices we have – about the work we do and how we spend our time?

20

Quitting, changing and crying

What happens when things don't work out exactly as planned, you get made redundant or you just like a bit of uncertainty? The job landscape is changing. The average millennial will change careers five to seven times during their working life, and around a third of the total workforce will change jobs every twelve months.

Here are some people who are doing things slightly differently. Not massively differently – none are living in the wilderness or have started communes, but they have made decisions that might raise the eyebrows of a careers advisor.

Meet Lotte Jeffs

Lotte is a journalist. She's a brilliant writer and has been published in the *Independent*, the *Guardian*, the *Sunday Times*, the *Evening Standard* and *ELLE*. She was deputy editor of *ELLE* magazine and spent six months as its acting editor-in-chief before taking redundancy. She is now exploring a career in advertising but is very much still a journalist and is working on her first book. After being made redundant, Lotte jumped industries. Here she tells us about the advantages to seeing an old beloved industry from the outside ... and reassessing her worth.

On redundancy from ELLE

Because my job and job title was so intrinsic to my sense of self, it felt like such an emotional experience. To just have that pulled from under me was very psychologically challenging. Perhaps if I had been doing a job I didn't care about that much, or didn't feel that personally involved with or attached to it might have been easier.

On your job title being your identity

Whatever work I do for brands or agencies, I still feel like being a magazine editor and journalist is what defines me. When you're in a certain world [fashion and magazines] you end up feeling so much of your value and interest as a person is tied up with your profession. I probably shouldn't have taken so much sense of my worth from my job.

On the positives of moving industries

I definitely value myself professionally more now that I know my skills are transferable and know how to monetise them. Working commercially for brands is such a different industry to independent publishing, with such a different pay scale.

On salary

In journalism I remember really fighting for a pay rise of 1 or 2 grand and then being on £35,000 for so long. My salary improved considerably when I went to ELLE but even then I was struggling financially slightly. The pay is better at all levels in advertising than in journalism, and working in this industry has made me reassess the value of my skills and experience.

Meet Naomi Oluleye

The panel event 'The Power of Quitting' was started in London by Naomi, and it proved so popular that it's been rolled out to New York and Berlin. It's a celebration of rebellious women who have made their careers their own, those who have quit big jobs, have been made redundant or completely pivoted careers. The real pull of her events is that nothing in the room is left unsaid: being a shitty mum, closing down your business, being underpaid and even being very well paid.

Naomi is about to go full-time at Bumble Business after three years of freelancing. I love Naomi's career story for a few reasons: one, she helps people celebrate negatives as strengths; two, she has recently gone from freelance into full-time work, which we don't hear about nearly as often as stories of people going from full-time to freelance; three, wait until you hear her brilliantly diligent way of working out current freelance rates.

Naomi on asking people what they earn

When I went freelance, I had no idea what to charge or what my day rate should be, so I spoke to as many people as possible. I started with ex-work colleagues, mainly people more senior than me, who I had worked with in the past. I asked them what my average day rate should be and what they were paying people with similar experience. Then I spoke to recruiters, because I wanted to make sure I wasn't pricing myself out of the market. It was important to me to make sure I was competitive, as it's easy to price yourself out of good work.

I was very open and willing to share my rate, and would ask others theirs. I created a Google Doc of freelancer fees, so whenever anyone told me a day rate I'd add it to a Google Doc with their industry, their role, level of seniority and workplace. Before, I had no idea what a designer should be paid, or if PR agencies paid the same rates as social agencies, so I've built up a data set of around fifty people in different industries and different skill sets and what those people are being paid. Obviously I used it to make sure I was getting the best rate, but it also really helps when staffing a project, as I now know how far a budget will go. The most interesting thing I saw from making that doc was how often people at a junior level were underpricing themselves. Perhaps they don't know or they're too scared to ask, but that was the definite commonality I saw.

On awkward conversations

Ex-colleagues who were more senior than me were very open and willing to share details and rates, but where I found people more 'iffy' was when talking to peers. When I was freelancing in-house at agencies, people would be weird about disclosing what they were getting, as they felt competitive. One of the negatives about freelancing is that there is a feeling that there isn't enough work for everyone, even when there is. Whenever anyone did tell me their day rate they always added a caveat or an excuse, like, 'It's £400 per day but I negotiated that around X or Y …'

On downtime between jobs

At first I'd get the worst anxiety. What should I be doing? I'd be like, 'Oh my god I'm so unemployable.' I noticed that my panics and freak-outs were completely linked to my worth. If I was working I was the happiest person ever, and if I wasn't working I was down. It's why I started my events, because I need to be doing something. I thought I should use downtime to promote myself and do work that I was really passionate about.

Before I would wonder why I was feeling so down; now I know it's because I'm not working, and when I'm not working I don't feel validated. Do I think it's a positive that a lot of my worth comes from work? Not necessarily. But it is part of me. And it is a part of society; people care and judge you on what you do. Even when freelancing everyone asks, 'What clients do you work for? What projects are you doing?'

On going back into full-time

I'll miss not being able to go on holiday, but then I guess as a freelancer I found it hard to go away. I'll miss being able to dial up my earnings by working really hard or choosing to earn less and have a relaxed month.

On advocating for yourself

When discussing my full-time role at Bumble I've made sure I can still do my own events. I think if I hadn't been independent I wouldn't have known how to negotiate for myself, but after being freelance I know how I work best, what I need and what I want to be paid. When you step out [of full-time work] you learn so much about yourself, and you learn what you can ask for, so I'm returning to a full-time job feeling empowered.

Meet Rebecca

Rebecca worked as a paralegal and then as a lawyer in large multi-national hedge fund firm for many years, ending up earning £130k plus bonuses before quitting to go travelling for nine months. Back in London she's been a painter and decorator and now works in the civil service, earning a salary of approximately £45k.

On learning to respect money

I could never have quit my hedge-fund salary and then go straight into £45k. Travelling gave me a different relationship with money and taught me a different lifestyle. I have a better sense of money, mainly because I ran out of it and had to live on very little for a time.

On using money to 'feel like herself'

When I first started travelling, I would use money to feel like myself again. If I was lonely I'd take myself out for expensive food in order to make myself feel better. It was interesting, as I noticed I was conditioned to think 'It will be OK if I can go out for a nice meal.' I had to learn how to self-sooth without money. The things I found pleasure in before were usually giving myself luxuries, rather than, say, going for an amazing walk.

On knowing her privilege

It was frightening having no job, but also as a capable woman with qualifications and transferable skills I knew I could go and get a job doing anything and be all right; I have always known ever since I got my first job at 16 that I was employable, and I would be OK doing whatever. When I got back from travelling I had to take lots of different jobs – in the last year I've packed goody bags in Westfield, I've painted and decorated, nannied … Even when I had no money, no job and nowhere to live I never felt destitute because I always knew I could work.

On bad habits

I never really told anyone this, but before I left the hedge fund, I would spend £20k a year on a credit card, and pay it off with part of my bonus at the end of the year and then start again. And I was paying 29.5 per cent APR most of the time. I knew the bonus was coming, so I was like, 'I am just pre-spending my money.' I feel like such a dick now as I could have saved so much money. But I was such a dickhead because money didn't have any value to me then. I was very lavish with gifts – everyone would get a £50 or £100 gift, I would take champagne to everything I went to even if it was the opening of someone's fucking door. And you attract different people – I had one of those bloodsucker boyfriends when I was a rich straight woman and they would take so much of my money.

On never escaping the money conversation

The civil service is the most inclusive place I have ever worked. Everyone wears rainbow lanyards to ally themselves with me and my other queer colleagues. We have very open discussions about mental health; there are mental health drop-in clinics, everyone is very conscious of how people feel, about leaving on time – it is a remarkable place. But even though the civil service strives not to be racist, sexist, homophobic, ableist, there is something called 'pay bandism'. Everything is judged by your pay band and people refer to their bosses like 'oh my PB7 [pay band 7] will have to sign that off'. Everyone knows everyone's pay band and people can be funny about talking to people a band below them – there is a real stigma about low pay bands.

Meet Missy Flynn

Missy founded the restaurant Rita's in 2013 with her partner and two friends. Rita's shot to success, received rave reviews and became a major part of East London's nightlife. In 2016 Missy and her co-founders had to make the difficult decision to close the restaurant, as she wrote in an article for *The Debrief*: 'The decision to close was not an easy one. The restaurant had become very well loved, but impossible to maintain. Rising rent, overheads, staffing issues and tricky business partners meant that there came a point after four roller-coaster years that something had to give. I had to get off. I felt sick at the thought of it and I was dizzy for a long while afterwards. I desperately wanted at the time to find some strength to believe that if I kept giving it my all, all of the problems would disappear, but eventually, even positive thinking had to make way for a real solution to a very real problem.'

I spoke to Missy about her work and her life two years on from closing Rita's and how she feels about money and failure.

Missy on everyone else presuming you'll be a success

One of my only regrets is that I feel like I took myself out of paid work for many years. Earning money from opening a restaurant is hard. But people saw a packed restaurant, they saw that it was being reviewed in the press and I think they expected that to translate into financial success. I wish people hadn't expected that I would have loads of money all the time, because once people believe that, it's hard to then suddenly say, 'No, by the way we actually don't make any money.'

On the difficulty of pretending

Being more open about the fact that things had gone wrong took the sting out of the initial stigma of failing. It was hard to make the decision to close the restaurant, but to pretend that everything was 'all good' at the same time would have been very difficult. Sometimes the pretence is almost harder than the reality.

On focusing on the good things

I could focus on the fact that we had to close down our business, or I could see the fact that I started a restaurant in my twenties, built a brand, and learned how to push through, be resilient and take risks.

Meet Liv Siddall

Liv is a writer, editor and a contributing editor of *Riposte Magazine*, and has her own podcast, *Redundancy Radio*, where she interviews different guests about their jobs. It was through the podcast's success that I first heard of Liv. She was editor of *Rough Trade Magazine* for nearly two years before being made redundant in 2017. This is her story on dealing with the loaded word that is 'redundancy', how it feels when your job is taken away from you and turning negatives into positives.

Liv on not doing it for the money

I was on £25k doing about four people's jobs in one go, making a sixty-four-page monthly music magazine without a team, but I didn't really care because I was having such a good time – it was a dream job and for a time I was having the most fun ever. When they first offered me the job they were like, 'The salary is low but you know, in six months it will go up and then it will go up again in a year' and that was actually a lie. In the end they said, 'Your salary is never going to go up; it's never gonna grow.' So that wasn't cool, but again I was so happy [at Rough Trade] that I didn't really mind, and I was doing some extra freelance bits for money. Whenever I earned money from freelancing I always put that in a savings account. I went to New York for [Rough Trade] twice, and even then my expenses were about $10 a day to spend on food. I was like, 'That's a coffee and a muffin.' But I was used to not being wealthy, so I didn't really mind.

On losing the dream job

People loved it [*Rough Trade Magazine*], and as soon as it got to its very best, I was called into a meeting, and I was like, 'What, why are we having a meeting? We never have meetings', and I walked into the room and the HR lady was there, and the director, and I knew. I think I said, 'Oh my god, am I being fired?' and they said, 'Sit down. We can't afford to do the magazine any more because it is costing too much money. So you can either be the social media manager, or you have to leave', and I replied, 'Well, I am not trained to be a social media manager, and I have no interest in it at all', and they said, 'Well, then you are on your notice period.'

I remember walking out of the shop and I think I must

have looked upset because everyone was like 'Liv, Liv'. I just walked round the corner and sat on the pavement, and as I was walking along the street I was just crying and this woman with her kid and her husband came up to me and just held me, and she was like 'What's wrong?' and I was like 'I've lost my job.' I didn't know who to call or what to do and everything was just falling around me.

On losing more than a job

Oh my god, it was my whole identity. It was who I was, it was what I was doing, it was all my spare time, it was my work and my after work. It was who I was. I was so proud of what I was doing and I was so happy. My only gripes were minor, about the wage and sometimes about the management of the company. Apart from that it was just heaven.

On that word 'redundancy'

It was eighteen months ago that I was made redundant. I am kind of out of it now but last month I had this huge crisis where I wouldn't get out of bed and I was sort of depressed really. I didn't know what I was doing, I didn't know what path I was on. I was doing some corporate work and I was just so so miserable. I was in bed one day just lying there and my boyfriend asked, 'What's wrong?' and I said, 'I am having a crisis', and he told me, 'Do you realise that every month since you have been made redundant, this has happened?' and I hadn't realised. My confidence has been knocked – I'm actually paying for therapy now to work through it.

On making lemonade

But then, you know what? My friend pointed out to me the

other day, 'Did you realise what you did after you got made redundant? You turned that into business, you built on it and you made a podcast shouting about how you were made redundant.' There is a thing that I heard once, a theory based on changing a tyre. If you are driving along and you see someone on the side of the road and they have a burst tyre, if they are just waving at the traffic, people don't tend to stop, but if they are seen to be trying to fix it, people will more likely stop. So if you are seen to be trying I think people are really supportive of you. I remember putting out the redundancy radio podcast and thinking, 'No one is going to listen to this, it is just me chatting', but it's been really popular.

Meet Thomas Davies

Over the course of ten years Thomas worked his way through the ranks at Google, eventually becoming director of global partnerships at Google Cloud and earning a six-figure salary. In February 2017 he resigned after taking eight months of garden leave to consider his next move. He is now the founder and CEO of Temporall, a team of world-leading experts in organisational culture and performance.

Thomas on that 'What the fuck now?' moment

I remember one particular moment, sitting on the edge of my bed, thinking, 'Crap. I'm nearly 40 and I don't think I'm going to become a CEO.' I was working for Google – of course I was never going to become a CEO there. I kept finding myself questioning what I wanted to achieve in the next ten years. Did I just want to be three more rungs up the ladder in the same place? I realised the answer was no.

I'd travelled all around the world, and I just decided that the next time I did that it would be for me. It would be for my team and my business, because it was knackering.

On taking financial risk

I'd never written a cheque for £17k before, and frankly at times that felt like a betting slip. You're just hoping that, as a founder, you make enough good decisions every day to make it worthwhile. You constantly question your sanity – am I doing the right thing? – £17k isn't a lot of money in comparison to what I left behind and took off the table. The big thing is [leaving] a company with healthcare, pension and employee benefits. When you have all those things, and you have a decent salary, and potential for bonuses, that's not an easy thing to walk away from. Losing the predictability was hard, and you have to figure out whether you can afford to lose that. I've always been quite careful with money.

On really wanting it

There's no hiding when you're the founder. You can't blame anyone else. There's no off switch. I work seven days a week, and I choose to do that.

On getting out of your comfort zone

Over a six-to-nine-month period, I must have had coffee with about 200 people. I'm a natural introvert, but I forced myself to ask people I met for advice, and contacts I could talk to. If you want inspiration and ideas, that method was a gift.

On defining success

I'm not motivated by the money. My children grew up

knowing that their dad worked at Google, and I would hear them talking about it in the playground. If I can get my company – reputationally, brand-wise – to a point where my children can say, 'My dad founded Temporall', and the person they're telling says, 'Oh, I know that company', that would be cool. If my children say, well done Dad, you stepped out of 'the big G' and did something for yourself, that's good enough for me.

21

Working for free

Interning for free

Let's first understand what the government classes as an intern:

> An intern is classed as a worker and is due the National Minimum Wage if they're promised a contract of future work. They're only classed as a voluntary worker (and therefore don't have to be paid the minimum wage) if they're working for a charity, voluntary organisation, associated fundraising body or a statutory body. The employer doesn't have to pay the minimum wage if an internship only involves shadowing an employee, i.e. no work is carried out by the intern and they are only observing.

Well, I can name a few companies that are breaking the law right now. Interning for free or basic expenses is rife in the 'creative industries'. Magazines, design studios and fashion labels can be partly run by unpaid workers. And those unpaid workers are all there with the intention of impressing and getting a job, so definitely fall into the government's category of 'promised a contract of future work', even if that contract has stipulations like being a one-in-a-million talent or having a famous dad.

According to the Sutton Trust, a social mobility charity, about 70k internships are given each year in the UK. It estimates that out of 10k graduates who are in internships six months after they leave university, a fifth are unpaid. The Trust calculated the cost of doing an unpaid internship as more than £1k a month in London and £827 in Manchester, which obviously means valuable work experience isn't accessible to those from families on low and middle incomes. The practice of unpaid internships definitely makes for a less diverse workforce across many industries.

As one writer currently interning at a magazine told me, 'All of the other interns including myself come from a pretty privileged background, and although we might work in a bar in the evening and I'm handing out flyers in front of Tube stations for a few hours a week, our parents help us pay the rent. Notably, right now everyone in the office is white.'

It's an unfair system, but it shouldn't be on the interns to affect the change. It's on those in power to call out the problem. But we know that's not happening enough. A spokesperson for Condé Nast, the publisher of *Vogue*, told the *Guardian* – 'those undertaking workplace shadowing were "in the office to learn, are entirely free to attend external meetings and interviews, and are not obliged to come to the office every day". The publisher was therefore under no obligation to pay the national minimum wage but did give some travel expenses.' This is incredibly frustrating, as it ignores the fact that interns are willing to bust their asses for free to impress someone who can give them a job, and if someone did casually leave to attend an interview during office hours they would most likely be judged as 'not very committed' and therefore not considered for a paid position.

How to fight a ridiculous, unfair system

- Don't be afraid to email organisations that normally only offer unpaid work experience (Condé Nast evidently being one of them) and ask if they offer provisions to those who can't afford to work for free, to break into their industry.

- If the only thing you'll take away is the name of the company and coffee-making skills, then you don't need to spend too much time there. Learn who the key people are and leave. You can use the company's name to get into the next place and you haven't lost anything.

- Don't spend longer than six weeks at an organisation working for free, and only stay that long if you're learning new skills. Six weeks is long enough to name the place on your CV and long enough for them to know whether they want to pay you.

- Use their name straight away. The moment you get in the door start emailing other companies to say, 'I'm working at X at the moment but was wondering if you knew of any opportunities ...' It's always easier to ask for help/seek new work when you have something going on.

- Ask if the internship could be part-time so you can work during the other days of the week. Being somewhere for two days a week for ten weeks is more beneficial than being somewhere for two weeks solid. That way you can balance it with paid work too.

- Tell people you are looking for paid work. If you chat to someone at the printer and they ask your role, make sure you say, 'I'm interning, but I really hope to get hired.' Sometimes people who hire interns start to think of it as a service to the intern, like, 'we're doing them a favour', and they forget the end goal.

- Ask when they last hired an intern. If never, get out of there.
- Only stay if you are learning something. A full-time unpaid internship that leaves you in debt and with no new skills is a step backwards, not forwards.
- If you have a paid position at a company that doesn't pay their interns, challenge their policy of unpaid internships. Many industries have their own initiatives where a collection of companies all sign up to a fair intern scheme; see if your industry has one and present this to your employers.
- If you can afford to work for free, question whether you should be helping to normalise a practice (particularly in the creative industry) that means those who actually need to earn money from their craft can't.

What about panels, speaking or judging awards?

The irony of someone asking a woman to be on a panel titled 'How to ask for what you are worth' and offer no fee is not lost on me. I will sometimes talk on a panel for free though – if it's something I care about, I enjoy it and it can be really great exposure. But not if it's a corporate gig. I last spoke at a Facebook event, and they asked my fee to which I sceptically replied '£250?' and they said, 'No, we can pay £500', which made me think, 'What could I have asked for?!' This proves that if it is a corporate gig you should 100 per cent ask for a fee. If they are making money off you, then surely you should get some of that.

Mainly though I'm offered the currency of 'exposure'. When I was working full-time I was much more likely to judge awards or speak for free, since my mortgage was guaranteed to be paid by my salary, but now that I'm freelance I have to consider what paid work I might miss out on by dedicating time to a speaking gig or a TV appearance.

The way I make my decision on which opportunities to say yes to is how excited I am to be asked. If it feels like a ball-ache and I'm not going to be paid then I say no. With any request for an interview, a panel, a TV appearance I always ask, 'Is there a fee?' The wording of that sentence means that if there is no fee I am leaving myself the option of thinking about it and accepting later, or shutting it down immediately. I can decide based on how they respond.

Working for friends for free

'Friends ask me to do "a small thing as a favour" but that small thing is actual work.' A solicitor explains how it feels when friends ask her to look over documents or give free advice. 'If it's a really close friend and they ask when they know I'm not stressed that's fine, but sometimes I have to say no and it makes me feel uncomfortable.' The business of charging a friend is tricky and sometimes it's easier to say no. What people often forget when they ask a friend to do something is that their time is money. 'I've done my sister's wedding invite,' a graphic designer tells me. 'But everything else I say no to as if I'm going to work for free then it will be on my own projects and I don't even have time for them.'

A professional photographer told me that people often ask him to photograph something as a favour quite unthinkingly.

'They don't realise I don't just point a camera and shoot; there are days of planning that go into what I do.' A website builder explained how the most annoying thing was when people think they're doing him a favour by offering him a chance to do something creative … for free. 'If it's a huge opportunity and the exposure is going to be massive I might think about it, but chances are it's not – it's a mate setting up a vinyl store.'

'I used to be happy doing the odd bit of writing for friends when I was employed full-time,' a brand copywriter tells me, 'but now that I'm freelance it's different.' People often don't realise that you're actually asking more of a freelancer than someone in full-time employment, as their time isn't paid for by someone else. And they will most likely have a rate card for what you're asking them to do.

If you're in an industry or have a skill where you are often asked by friends to provide a professional service, then sit down and work out your own rules. Write down what you will and won't do and under what circumstances. No one ever has to see this, but you will have some clarity. It might be that you have a hard and fast rule that you will not work for friends.

Ask yourself how the request makes you feel. Be clear on what you can and can't do, especially if you are asked to do miscellaneous tasks like helping someone with their business plan. If you want to help but don't want to have to open up a PowerPoint presentation and read a shoddy proposal in your own time, say you can offer a thirty-minute coffee. You know if what someone is asking you feels like too much. Trust your instinct and don't be afraid to go back with a cost.

22

The freelance trap

I'd like to explain the freelance trap by talking about the price of a cat. A friend had chosen a rescue cat for his family. The appointment to pick up the cat was on a Tuesday afternoon, which meant he had to take the day off work. He joked that the cat had cost him £500, his day rate. I guess in a sense it had.

There is a danger with freelance to never say no to work and to start judging time against how much you could earn, a trip to see your mum = £200, a hangover = £150, going to your kid's sports day = £350. But this is no way to live.

Even the most successful freelancers get the freelance fear – that feeling that work will dry up, that you will become irrelevant and the money will stop coming in. The fear can lead people to say yes to everything, never carving out time for themselves, their family, their friends, and this can lead to burnout. The fear can make freelancers, who went self-employed for the very reason that they might take advantage of a sunny Tuesday afternoon every now and again, become less likely to take time off than when they were full-time.

Here are some tips to stop you from feeding the

freelance fear. Even if you aren't freelance, thinking about the economics of freelancing can help you with your own cyclical relationship with money, work and time.

More money isn't always more

Sometimes time off can be more financially valuable than money. Washing your clothes, ironing them and arranging them so you can see them clearly, all help curb that feeling of needing something new. Even having time to clean can help you save money – you're more likely to order takeout if you don't have a clean space to cook. Sometimes working too hard depletes all of our energy, leaving us lazy in other areas and costing us money.

Learn to say no

Once you reach capacity you must learn to say no. Think about why you went freelance in the first place; I'm sure it wasn't to work all the time.

Put aside days to stay on top of your finances

Half a day a month or a full day every couple of months should be set aside to go through all your finances: staying on top of invoices, chasing unpaid invoices, submitting expenses, budgeting, forecasting, liaising with your accountant or completing self-assessment – all takes time, and when you're freelance you're not paid for it. But that doesn't mean you should put it off or give preference to fee-paying clients. Not being on top of your finances costs money.

Don't pretend to work

To feel relevant and connected and to starve off the freelance fear, we often pretend to ourselves that we are working. We tinker with our portfolio, we rewrite the same piece of copy, we sit at our computers scrolling through social media saying we are 'researching'. Chaining yourself to your desk can make you less productive. Take breaks – throughout the day, the month and the year. Take note of when you are most productive. It's tempting to stay hustling when you don't have work that day, but freelancers have to get good at taking breaks when they are given them. You can't control the ebb and flow of work, but you can decide to not work every single day of the year.

Work for the amount of time you are booked for

If a client has booked you for two days, don't work over into the third day for fear that what you have done is not enough. I often find clients overestimating what someone can get done in a day or a week. When you first take the brief be realistic about how long the project may take, and if it's the kind of work that requires feedback from the client. Make sure you build this in when quoting and be strict about how many rounds of feedback the client gets so that a job doesn't bleed into more days than you are being paid for.

Get paid overtime

If someone offers you work you are too busy to take on and to fit it in you'll be working into evenings and the weekend then go back with a ridiculous price. If they say yes then at least you are overcompensated for what will technically be overtime.

Apply late fees on unpaid invoices

Twitter can be a great source of information – particularly if you don't work in an office with colleagues to confer with. One freelancer, Martha Sprackland, shared her invoice template footer on Twitter for other freelancers to use (printed below so you can copy it too), tweeting, 'This week I applied this to a late invoice and emailed the employer a new version with the increased fee. A mere two days later, it was paid in full plus late fee. Always works!' If all freelancers did the same, it could become standard rather than an awkward move – no one should be afraid of asking for money they have already earned. If you have freelance friends share this with them so we can make this a common practice, not just for the brave.

*Payment terms are 14 days. Please be aware that according to the Late Payment of Commercial Debts (Interest) Act 1998, freelancers are entitled to claim £40.00 late fee upon non-payment of debts after this time, at which point a new invoice will be submitted with the addition of this fee. If payment of the revised invoice is not received within a further 14 days additional interest will be charged to the overdue account at a statutory rate of 8% plus Bank of England base of 0.5%, totalling 8.5%. Parties cannot contract out of the Act's provision.

BE GOOD WITH MONEY

Just in case it's not abundantly clear (and by now it really should be), I am not a financial expert, and have not been accredited to give financial advice. In fact, the financial experts who know me personally, especially those who knew me in my twenties, would be horrified to think I was telling people what to do with their money.

I'm not going to tell you how to invest or when to buy a house. There's no point knowing any of that if you're still paying bank charges on your overdraft anyway. I am going to tell you how I went from debt to a savings account, and I'm going to share what I've learned from financial experts and normal people who have a healthy relationship with their money.

This is about working out what works for you using the information you have and the people you know. I'm just here to get you started.

23

Get financially fit – the wellness trend you actually need

There was a moment a couple of years ago when I realised that exercise is as important for my mind as it is for my butt. That was my first mini wellness revelation, and recently I've had another – getting financially fit will be the next wellness trend. Research has shown that the worse you feel about your finances, the worse you feel overall. Sorting out our finances will begin to be one of the things we do to protect our mental health. Like getting a good night's sleep or taking a break from social media.

We're clearly concerned about wellness: we're pouring money into it. The retail wellness industry in the UK alone is worth over £23bn. Alcohol consumption is going down, the number of people smoking has halved and gym membership are up. We have apps that track everything from menstrual cycles to our step count and their effects on our mood and well-being. Up to 24 million UK adults (46 per cent of us) pop vitamins daily. In 2016 'yoga' was one of the most Googled words. The corporate wellness industry is worth over $40m worldwide, with companies offering their employees sleep pods, rock climbing, flexible working

hours, decent parental leave, healthy grazing snacks and …
knitting clubs.

For all the work we're doing for our health, there is one
fact that the wellness industry currently overlooks: money is
the greatest source of anxiety. Study after study turns up data
that shows that money is the most common cause of stress
for every generation and both sexes. A twenty-two-country
survey by GfK conducted with 27,000 consumers found that
money is the main cause of stress for 29 per cent of people,
and the research psychologist Dr Galen Buckwalter found that
23 per cent of adults and 36 per cent of millennials experience
financial stress at levels that qualify as a diagnosis of PTSD.
An American study that looked into workplace wellness
trends asked over 500 employers to select the top medical
conditions that cost their company money: high cholesterol,
depression, anxiety, hypertension, high blood pressure, heart
disease and diabetes. These very same health problems are
exacerbated by financial stress. Stress has a very real, physical
effect on our bodies. When we're stressed we release high
levels of cortisol. It can also increase your heart rate, which,
when experienced regularly, can weaken the walls of your
arteries. Often a stressful experience is immediately followed
by a spike in blood pressure.

We've all felt that physical relief when our bank account
looks healthy. A report by the *Journal of Consumer Research*
found that when consumers asked themselves how they are
doing, their perceived financial well-being is a key predictor
of their overall well-being; if they felt financially secure,
chances are they'd feel well overall.

Worrying about money eats time, it curbs enjoyment, it
can keep you up at night and lead to sleep deprivation, it puts

strain on your relationships (with friends, family, partners and children) and leads to behavioural issues like drinking more, under- or overeating, withdrawing and 'checking out' of life. We need to start seeing financial health as crucial to our holistic well-being. The irony that we might spend £6 on a 'healthy' cold-press juice when we can't really afford it shouldn't be lost on anyone.

There are surface bubbles indicating a movement. This book is one of many zeitgeist money books. Fashion magazines like *ELLE* are dedicating issues to the subject, and cool collectives like Babyface and Women in Fashion are putting on money panels. The subject of money, of our money, what we earn, how we spend and how we feel about it, is punching high for millennial engagement and retention. It's no longer a boring topic sidelined to those who work in finance. We're realising that as long as we earn and spend money, financial health is a topic for all of us, and an interesting one too.

So how do we get financially fit? What even is the downward dog of personal finances? To truly feel financially healthy you should be spending less than you earn and have both short-term and long-term savings. If you're not there yet then working towards that is good enough. But how do we get there? Firstly, we need an honest relationship with our money, which starts with conversation. Without conversation shame and stigma stick to money. Only with education and conversation can we untangle the role money plays in our life and start making it work for us. Secondly, we need a plan. We're going to look at budgeting, auditing, spending, saving and dealing with debt in a moment. The best kind of money plan relies on lots of small habit changes, rather than a strict diet that you'll binge your way out of after two days. And just like you wouldn't run a marathon before you can run for the bus, you don't need to do everything all at once. It took me six years to get financially fit. I didn't decide to be good with money and wake up ready to budget, but instead made small changes that added up until I had myself sorted. This is what my progression looked like:

Year 1: Learned to budget

Year 2: Cleared debt

Year 3: Learned to save

Years 4 & 5: Ticked off some financial goals – mine was buying a flat, yours might be buying a car, going travelling, getting married or going freelance

Year 6: Planning for retirement (this is still a work in progress)

Your path might look shorter, or longer. Like following the running programme 'Couch to 5k', getting financially fit is a journey. And like running a race, it should be something to celebrate when you achieve it. The wellness industry encourages us to put so much energy and money into areas of our life where the results are minuscule: superfoods, gong baths, acupuncture, organic veg boxes, hot yoga. But perhaps the best thing to do for our health is to work out first if we can afford to do any of those things. A park run might beat a spin class.

Getting financially fit could change your life. Hey, it might even make your sex life better – stress doesn't do anything positive for our libido. It will help you sleep better, it will improve your relationships and, much like meditative thinking, it will give you daily peace of mind. Welcome to 2019's defining wellness trend: the financial health revolution. As Roman emperor Marcus Aurelius said, 'People look for retreats for themselves, in the country, by the coast, or in the hills … There is nowhere that a person can find a more peaceful and trouble-free retreat than in his own mind.' Financial well-being is clarity, it is mental health. So let's pull our metaphorical trainers on and get ready to budget, green juice optional.

24

The freedom of a budget

The word 'budget' conjures up negative feelings. I think of microwaving unappealing leftovers. I picture intense rounds of sums and admin. I feel the overbearing weight of FOMO. Being on a budget means staying in. It's boredom, it's restraint, it's not buying the posh yoghurt.

Conversely, it's freedom. It's mental health. It's being on top of things. It's owning your situation. It's setting your own terms. It's buying the posh yoghurt because you budgeted for it. It's saying no because saying yes will hit you harder. It's feeling smug.

'I've yet to find someone who doesn't understand the basics of money. One, spend less than you make. Two, save for the future. I don't know anyone who can't recite those two facts. But people still don't do them, and as a result I think people feel an intense amount of shame,' says financial therapist Brad Klontz. The rules of money management are actually pretty simple. That's why it's sometimes difficult to admit (even to ourselves) that we haven't done the most basic of things – kept to a budget. But we know by this point in the book that how and why we spend money doesn't just equate to how much money we have or don't have, or even our financial education. Instead it comes down to our emotions, our money scripts, who we hang out with and what our parents taught us.

Sticking to a money budget is like healthy eating, or exercising, or being on time: easy only in principle. In an ideal world we'd be putting some of our money away in savings and not blowing our monthly wages in the first weekend after getting paid. But it's not an ideal world. Let's remember financial therapist Eric Dammann's words, 'There is no right or wrong way to be with money.' He's right – you can be a spender or a saver, frugal or spendthrift, but there are two things I don't want anyone to feel about money: shame or stress.

If you never plan how you spend your money, chances are you feel one of those two things regularly. So what is a budget? A budget is knowing how much money you can spend.

Creating a money budget can feel like just another thing to fail at. 'I either go way over or way under – it's like dieting,' Lee, 34, tells me. 'I get hyper miserly or I fuck up and start bingeing. I'll "accidentally" buy some clothes I didn't really have the money for and then I think fuck it let's all drink negronis. Then I'll go completely the other way and see how many days I can get through and spend nothing. I'll cancel every subscription I have and renounce material needs. Is there a term for money bulimia?'

A friend tells me of her failed attempts to budget: 'I've not had money for so long that my whole life feels like one long budget. The last thing I want to do is spend time logging and thinking about my lack of funds. So yeah, I spend more than I have, I don't save, I don't earn enough: I do everything wrong.' Hearing people talk about budgets, it's no surprise that financial therapist Simonne Gnessen doesn't use the word. She believes it has too many negative connotations, and so instead says 'spending plan'. I'm going to stick to 'budget' though. I don't want to be scared of it.

For a long time I had no idea that people had 'budgets'. I never did any maths – not even the simplest of sums to work out what I would have left to spend after my bills and rent. Instead I relied on a feel for the kind of shops and restaurants I could afford to be in, which of course constantly failed me. My instinct told me to get out of Waitrose, and that Morrisons was probably fine. It didn't tell me not to buy the imported beer and prawn cocktail Pringles though. I always managed to spend more than I had coming in, and presumed everyone spent money like I spent mine, carrying on until they weren't allowed to spend any more, i.e. their card got blocked. But then I learned that people did sums and filled out Excel documents. Some had savings accounts! With actual money in them. They chose when to spend their money rather than their banks telling them when they couldn't.

Budgeting should feel like a heady mix of flow and control. It should be liberating and empowering rather than limiting. I've had many conversations with people about their money – how much they have, how they spend and how they feel about it. My biggest takeaway is that having more money doesn't necessarily make you happier, but having a healthy relationship with money and a sense of control does. Those who knew what they could spend and who had made peace with the amount of money they had, had greater freedom than those who were spending mindlessly.

When I spoke to a 27-year-old who earns £16k and had saved enough in the last year to go on holiday to Australia, I asked her how she did it. 'I budget, and every time I came across something I could spend my money on I thought to myself, "Is this worth more than going to Australia next year?"' I spoke to another 27-year-old, one who earns £50k, and they said 'there's no way' they could afford to go to Australia. The £50k earner also told me, 'I don't know where all my money goes, I never budget.'

Having a budget and sticking to it feels good. It's a clean, refreshed feeling, like sending a birthday card on time, or getting into a freshly changed bed. I'm not going to prescribe a budgeting form for you to fill out, nor is there an Excel document linked to this book. I'm not giving you a budgeting technique. It's more of a thought process gleaned from both the advice of many financial experts and the behaviour of normal people who have found peace with money.

Ultimately, like Simonne says, budgeting is a spending plan. It is a way for you to decide how to spend your money. Don't think about the restriction, think about the spending. Ask yourself, 'What do I want to spend my money on?'

How to budget

First things first – how much money do you actually have to spend?

Here's how you work it out:

1. Look at your payslip – what do you get each month after tax, pension and your student loan repayment has been deducted? This is your take-home salary.

2. Look at all of your regular bills and add them up: your rent, utility bills, loan or credit card repayments, standing order to Spotify, your usual travel expenses and that gym membership you keep meaning to cancel (in fact if there is anything you're paying for that you could easily live without, this is the moment to cancel it). What do you have left? This is the actual money you're working with each month. That is your budget.

3. Think of all the things you need to buy with that money: food, clothes, going out to Shanie's birthday party, a Mother's Day present, hair serum … Now you need to prioritise that budget so you have money for the things you want or need to do.

Talk to your friends

Ask them, 'Do you have a budget?' 'How do you prioritise what to spend your money on?' The greatest thing about breaking the taboo and talking about money is the sharing of information and tips. I asked my own friends and found the small spending tips they shared were actually huge penny-drop moments for me. A close friend told me that he eats a bowl of pasta before coming to the pub, 'so I don't get tempted to order a burger'. Another friend has deleted every app that allows him to spend money too easily: no Deliveroo, no Amazon and no Uber. It made me realise I could save money and still do many of the things I already do. I just have to make small adjustments. If I'd read advice like that on a banks blog or even in a book like this, I would probably have rolled my eyes and thought how restrictive that seemed, but knowing a friend I respect does it, well it has a different effect: I totally absorb that information. That's the power of speaking to friends first – getting a range of ideas and finding out what works for them (and might work for you).

Look at how you've spent in the past

We are always more optimistic about the future than we are about the present. We presume that by the time we have to wear that two-piece to the beach we'll have lost five pounds. We take the book *Sapiens* on another holiday despite it sitting in our suitcase unread for the last two trips. We believe naïvely that a better version of us exists in the future, yet it's not as simple as saying, 'I will never drink again', or 'I will only spend the money I earn'; to change our behaviour we have to strategise.

Looking at where the hell your money has gone in the past helps. New challenger banks like Monzo and Starling have easy-to-use apps that organise your accounts so you can see exactly what you are spending, so there's no more lying to yourself. I went through my bank statements from the last year with a highlighter pen, and I looked through my wardrobe, Instagram photos, Amazon and ASOS orders. In amongst the relentless £20 PayPals and numerous £5 Ubers when I evidently could have walked, there were stand-out items and memories. I am really glad I spent nearly £400 on a pair of shoes which three years later I have just had resoled for the second time: I love them. Flights? Every single time worth it, but the £20 I saved by getting the 5.55 a.m. flight? Not worth it. My yearly pilgrimages to large department stores to buy make-up and face cream still make me feel good thinking of them.

And then there are all the things I've spent money on

that I could live without. Apart from some cable ties and audiobooks, nothing I bought from Amazon improved the quality of my life (hello, owl-shaped sponges). I also realised how often I spent money on things I think I should spend my money on but that ultimately didn't bring me much pleasure – organic veg boxes that rotted at the bottom of my fridge, or meat from the posh butchers. I'm an average cook, so spending money on ingredients is a waste for me – every time I have bought a good piece of fish I've fucked it up. I used to think block-booking yoga classes would make me go to them, but in reality it just guarantees I'll waste more money, so now I never book an exercise class in advance.

Look at your bank balance

If you don't track your money, you can't budget. This is literally the key to every single budgeting technique – *looking* at your bank balance. If you don't know what you have, how do you know what you can spend? Mental addition doesn't work. We lie to ourselves or omit things like that second round of drinks. Look at your account every couple of days and acknowledge to yourself how much you have spent and on what.

It should not feel scary to look at your bank balance. The more you don't want to look, the more imperative it is that you look. Nothing is scarier than not knowing.

Work out your daily number

For the budget-averse, a really simple budgeting technique is to calculate your daily number. Work out how much money you have left each month after your bills have come out and you've put any savings away. Then divide that number by the number of days in the month. That is your daily budget. If you spend over it, you can work out your new daily budget by doing the same sum again; just take what money you have left and divide by the number of days in the month that are left.

Only budget what you have

This is a rule every freelancer needs to truly embrace. If it's not in your bank account don't class it as your money yet, even if you've earned it and invoiced for it.

Get a budget buddy

This is important. If you're cutting back, tell your friends. They might join you, they'll hopefully make accommodations for your new budget and they might be relieved themselves. What they're probably not going to do is judge. There's something noble about someone getting their act together. Tell them why – 'I need to buy a new laptop', 'I need to pay off debt', 'I've always wanted to go to Japan.' That way you only have to explain once rather than come up with an excuse every time. You never know, your friends might join you in your budgeting. An accountability buddy makes it much easier – challenge a best friend, a sibling or your partner to budget with you.

Fuck up, change up

Spark plugs go, needy friends invite you to expensive birthday meals, your electricity bill arrives on the same day as the council tax, somehow you spend a week's worth of money on a Friday night. You fuck up, and when you do it's really tempting to think, 'Budgets don't work. I can never stick to one. This is impossible.' But it's not. Just accept the blip and redo your budget with what you have left rather than letting a bad day, week or even month send you into a spiral. Budgeting is always a work in progress. Even great budgeters might need to change things up every month.

And that's budgeting

Look at your money, make plans for your money and note when you fuck up. Knowing you can spend within your means is empowering. It's liberating. You will feel clean, like you've gone for a run and grown your own vegetables. Try it.

How to shop

Practise mindful spending

I used to live with a friend who would constantly spend money on things she already had: another mascara, another black dress, more 'going out tops' than she had nights out (yet still had 'nothing to wear'). Mindless spending will fill your life with stuff, but if you haven't really thought about it, and don't really love it, then you'll still find yourself wanting more.

Mindful spending should be much more of a thing. Mindful spending means thinking about why you are spending. It is considering the consequences of purchasing an item. Mindful spending is being present in the moment and choosing to spend money rather than mindlessly handing over your card.

Really love your things

If less stress is the first positive to come from taking control of your spending, then the second is a greater love for things.

'The most financially healthy person is the person who has the ability to connect their money with the things that make them happy,' says financial advisor Simon Russell. There are multi-billion-dollar industries whose sole aim is to make us spend money we don't have on things we don't want. It takes perseverance, strategy and willpower to beat the consuming machine and only bring into our lives the things we truly want and have the time and space to appreciate.

When I buy something I ask myself a few key questions:

What could I do with this money instead?
Why am I buying this?
Do I have anything similar already?

Say I'm in Topshop and want to buy a £40 jumper. I ask myself, 'What could I do with this money instead?' I think through the things I haven't let myself buy in recent weeks – I weigh up the jumper versus perfume versus a babysitter. I also think about whether that money would make me feel better if it was sitting in the bank in case something extra special came up – a better jumper, perhaps, or it could be put towards a car, or I could save it and feel mentally sound.

The second question, 'Why am I buying this?', makes me question my mood. Am I looking for a pick-me-up? And if so, what could I do instead? Perhaps a £1 cookie would do the job. This question also makes me think about how I ended up in Topshop holding this jumper. If I'm only there because I have a meeting in the building next door and have twenty minutes to kill then that jumper has to be effing amazing.

The question 'Do I have anything similar already?' is really important. We've been conditioned to consume, and perhaps somewhere in our tribal brain we think stockpiling is a good idea. But in a land of plenty, hoarding isn't practical or sensible. I've often caught myself thinking, 'Oh I love these jeans, I must buy more like them.' Which is frankly ridiculous. What I should really think is, 'I love these jeans, I should wear them more often.'

And finally … if you're happy with your answers to the questions, then buy the goddamn jumper. Enjoy it!

Write a list

When you go to buy something or feel a 'want', rather than buying it straight away, add it to a list. I bet within a week or two there are things on that list that you no longer want and things that you would like but have realised you (evidently) can live without. Try this technique, please. It's such a simple way to not fill your house up with crap. You'll be surprised by how persuasive that initial impulse to buy something is, and how differently your thought process can be when you consider something rationally away from the place of purchase (even closing a tab on your computer).

Only buy something once you can truly say you're more excited about it than anything else on the list.

Watch your triggers

If every time an H&M email comes in you click on it and buy something, if you can't help but 'shop now' when Zara comes up in your Instagram feed, then the answer is happily simple: unsubscribe, block, unfollow. Remove all one-click purchases from your computer. Go to Google autofill and delete your credit card information. Sometimes just putting another five minutes in-between you and a purchase can stop a mindless splurge.

Also, watch how often we consume just to feel OK. When I'm working in an office, I often buy a coffee when I don't really want one. I enjoy the ritual of walking to the coffee shop, of clutching a warm coffee between two hands and strolling for a moment. Buying a coffee feels purposeful, and gives me a legitimate excuse for taking a break. Yet I could just have easily gone for a stroll, looked at the sky, enjoyed the fresh air – and not bought a coffee – and probably felt as refreshed.

The more you earn the more you spend

Watch out for the creep in your spending. OK, sometimes the more you earn the more you have to spend. A position and a pay rise might come with an unsaid rule that it's time you didn't wear scuffed shoes to work. But be really aware of 'keeping up' and of spending your money in a way you think you should rather than how you want to. I once joined in with my friends who were ordering crates of nice wine because I thought that's what people did, as they earned more money. I don't even like wine.

25

Save yourself – why saving is the best present you'll ever give yourself

Once you have learned to budget and live within your means, you can start thinking about saving and truly getting financially fit.

I never found the idea of a 'rainy day' inspiring enough to get me to save money. The idea of money sitting in an account in case bad things happened instead of using it for fun things right now seemed, well, just so boring.

Savings looked like wasted money (the irony being that I didn't see paying interest on my overdraft as wasted money). I couldn't connect with what it would feel like to have spare money in the bank. In the game of money, saving felt like level ten, and I hadn't passed the other nine levels yet: not spending more than I had, getting out of debt, etc. I thought saving was something rich people did, people who had more money than they knew what to do with. Even as my salary increased, my mindset didn't change: I wasn't there yet. But it never feels like you're there yet. I, like so many people I've spoken to, believed there was plenty of time in the future to save, and that I would only be 22 once. I still had the same attitude at 32.

In the UK, roughly a quarter of adults with household incomes below £13,500 have more than £1k in savings. Saving doesn't come from having money – as we know, even people with a lot of money can find something to spend it all on every month. Saving rarely happens by accident. Saving happens when people mark that money as a cushion or for a big-ticket item, and deliberately put it aside. Not everyone can save in the short-term – your salary might not be enough to cover the basics, or you might be paying off debt – but remember that getting financially healthy is a project that takes years, not weeks.

While I haven't seen evidence that more money correlates with being happier, it does seem that a lack of money correlates with misery and stress. Savings free you from financial worry. Every day they provide a feeling of well-being. I now know I get greater contentment from being on top of my finances than I do from cocktails or shoes. I also know time spent batch-cooking meals to save money is preferable to giving that time to money-anxiety.

How to save

Pay off debt before you save

This is very important, so I'm going to use the words of the ultimate money expert, Martin Lewis. On MoneySavingExpert.com he advises, 'Pay debts off, possibly even including your mortgage, before you save. Forget the old "must have an emergency savings fund" logic as getting rid of debts beats that too.' Debt will always cost you more than you'll ever make in interest on savings.

Apart from student debt

The only exception to this rule is student debt. Student loans have no real interest cost (you tend to pay the equivalent of inflation), and are impossible to default on as repayments are deducted at source. Unlike normal loans, which require payment regardless of your situation, with student loans you don't need to repay them unless you're earning over a set amount. This applies even if you have started paying and then your income drops. As Martin Lewis says, 'This is crucial for deciding whether to repay. Firstly, it means if times get tough – you lose your job or your income drops – then unlike any other lenders, the student loan company won't come knocking on your door. You quite simply don't need to repay.' And – if you never earn over the threshold the debt is wiped after thirty(ish) years.

Don't wait to be brilliant

Waiting to become the kind of person who saves isn't a plan. We often have a misguided idea of adulthood, that as we get older we'll become more sensible, more boring and suddenly start saving. Or perhaps we think we'll save when we have more money, forgetting that all we've ever done when we've got more money is spend it.

I asked financial advisor Simon Russell how he persuaded his clients to save. He said a change in financial attitude rarely came after advice from others, and that normally it took a life-changing event – like a redundancy, a death or having a baby – to shake up someone's relationship with money. Annoyingly, I can attest to that: I only started saving when I went back to work after having my son and realising I wanted to leave my corporate job for the unstable world of journalism. At that moment what I wanted – to quit my job and try another career – was worth more than any other purchase. Since then, because it was a necessity, saving and living within my means has become a way of life, and I wish it hadn't taken giving birth to realise this. Mainly because I could have lived many more years stress-free.

'If you want £10k you have to start with a pound,' Bola Sokunbi, founder of Clever Girl Finance, says. It's true, to have money in the bank you have to start saving something at some point. If you're waiting to have loads of spare money then you'll never save. Start small and it will grow. Having healthy savings is not about having hundreds or thousands to put away in one go.

Automate

You've heard this a million times but I'm going to say it again. On the day you get paid, automatically put a set amount away into a savings account. If you're freelance make it a percentage of each invoice, and if you're paid monthly set up a direct debit so you never even see the money. Don't make it a monthly ordeal, and don't make it something you can choose to opt out of. Choose an amount that after three months will add up to a sum that you will be proud of. It should be enough that you can look at what you have achieved and feel proud, but not so much that it feels unattainable.

Don't aim too high

If you aim to save too much you will end up dipping back into your savings by the end of every month and feel like you've failed. Instead chose a reasonable amount that you believe you can stick to (start with an amount that only requires one lifestyle change).

Reward yourself

Is there an item or an experience that you really want? What do you desire? Think, plot, let your mind wander. Set up a savings account for that one thing. And name the account the thing you're saving for (your bank can do this, and apps like Starling have this feature built in). If you're saving for a few things, set up multiple savings accounts. You might have 'Long-term savings goals', 'Croatia' and 'Christmas' as savings accounts.

Trick yourself

I use software that disables my Internet to write undisturbed – and we can use similar tech to trick ourselves into saving. There are loads of apps, such as Revolut, that round up every purchase you make to the nearest pound and pop that money into a savings account. So say you spend £5.60 at Tesco – the app takes 40p and pops it into a savings account. This isn't necessarily the best way to save for the long-term, but it's a good start, and it might be the thing to make you realise that even you can save money.

Tell your friends

I know I've already said this, but again – share your goals with your friends. Petra, 35, who wanted to buy a flat in London, told me that 'when I decided that it really was time to own a place of my own I knew my social life would be the first thing hit by my savings plan. So I told my friends, "Look, I can't do that meal out/join you in the pub/ have brunch. I'm saving for a deposit." Turns out rather than making excuses, telling them went down really well. They understood; some wanted to start saving too. They'd come to my flat for dinner rather than meeting in the pub. With both the honesty and the saving money, I felt we were adults finally, at 35.'

Even if your friends aren't as positive and accommodating as Petra's, at least by telling them you don't have to come up with an excuse every weekend. Also by saying your savings goal out loud, you're accountable to someone.

Have them where you can see them

Savings are like a gold-star chart for adults: your own proof that you're brilliant. Open up your banking app and have a look at them – there in black and white you will see your willpower, what you can make happen if you commit to change. I look at my savings an unhealthy number of times considering they rarely change, but they give me a warm, smug feeling when I see them.

Fuck off fund

If you have nothing to fall back on then you're trapped in the life you're living right now. Change often costs money – whether it's having a buffer for the first rocky months of freelancing or being able to pay for the moving van when you split up with your partner. Everyone should feel empowered to sometimes make the difficult, expensive decision, and a 'Fuck off fund' will give you that.

Three months

Experts say you should have enough money in the bank so that you could survive for three months if your income stopped. That's enough to pay your rent or mortgage, your bills and your food. Work out what that number is then aim for it. If you can, when you're working out your budget, put savings in as a priority.

Plan ahead

You know the things coming up in the year ahead that will cost money. Christmas, summer holidays, maybe most of your friends have their birthdays in one month (you might have a thing for Libras). Save for these things. Don't act all, 'I didn't plan for this' when you knew all along it was coming.

26

Don't plan to die

'Tell me when you're going to die and I'll tell you how much you should save.' Royston, a charming financial advisor, says this is his standard reply to the very common question he gets from his clients: 'How much should I have in my pension?'

'One thing is for certain,' he continues. 'If you're not saving anything then I'm going to presume you're planning on dying early.'

For everyone that has ever put off paying money into their pension, no one else is going to do it for you, and the really hard thing to acknowledge is that because of compound interest, the earlier we put money away the more it will be worth by the time we need to draw from our pension. In an attempt to hammer this into my head, financial therapist Simonne Gnessen asked me:

If you started with a penny and it doubled every day, what would you have in 30 days' time?

A) £60
B) £32,008
C) £5,368,709.12

The answer is C. You can see why financial advisors trot this out to demonstrate the power of saving sooner. If you give your money time to grow, you won't have to put as much away. 'Forty-seven-year-olds constantly enter my office panicking because they have no pension,' Royston tells me. 'At that age they have to start putting away a third of their salary to get a decent pension together. But a 30-year-old can put a smaller percentage away and it will make a difference.'

MoneyAdviceServices.org.uk has an easy-to-use pension calculator. My results were sobering. I thought contributing £300 a month was enough (I'm 35 and started this year), but apparently that will mean when I retire I'm on track to live off £6k a year, and that doesn't even adjust for inflation. From the sea of information on how much we should all be saving there is one common rule. If when you retire you would like to live off half your current salary, then the percentage you should save should be *at least* half your age from when you started saving. So a 20-year-old should save 10 per cent, a 30-year-old should save 15 per cent, and a 40-year-old 20 per cent.

The government has recognised a huge problem: that most people are not saving for retirement, and that people are living longer. They've now made paying into a pension mandatory if you're aged 22 and over and earning over £11k. The new auto-enrolment initiative requires companies to have a staff pension scheme, and stipulates the contributions that employees and employers must make each month. But this doesn't cover freelancers.

If you are literally at the starting line with your pension, then a financial advisor, your bank or your accountant can help set you up with one. If in doubt, MoneySavingExpert. com will always point you in the direction of key pension providers.

Let's not plan to die. The earlier we start saving, the less money we have to put away. And you know what? Even if I die tomorrow and don't get to spend the money I put away for my pension, I'd still be glad I'd done it, because it makes me feel calm and serene *now*.

Find your lost pensions

If you think you have paid into a pension in the past but can't remember which company holds your pension, use the Gov. uk tracker service. It finds lost pensions and is super simple to use – you just put your place of work in and the years you worked there. It will tell you the company who managed your pension and give you a contact number and address. It's estimated that there are £3bn worth of lost pensions lying around unclaimed.

Do your own pension audit

Check your payslips to see what you're currently paying. Ask your workplace, if you increase your payment, do they up their contribution? Have a chat with your office finance department – what advice/information do they have on your company scheme? Can you arrange to get the pension manager into your office for an 'Ask me anything' session?

Don't expect a quick fix – the big things can take years

Clearing my debt took a year. Buying a flat with my boyfriend took nearly two years from deciding we should try to holding a set of keys. This year I will get myself in a good place for retirement. I now know that big financial goals aren't things you can sort out in a bank in an afternoon. They require commitment, often lots of small changes and always lots of forms. Understanding that things take a long time means you're less likely to fold when it becomes hard or boring. Getting a pension might be an hour on the phone to Standard Life, but be prepared for it to be difficult and stick with the challenge. Your future self will thank you …

27

This is debt

In case you've flipped to this section of the book because you're scared and in a lot of debt, I am going to start with these words because I want you to know that it is OK: 'Some people reading this will be in real difficulty and – because we don't talk about debt – won't have told anyone about their situation. So one thing I would encourage them to do is to get some debt advice. It's free, and no debt problem is *ever* unresolvable.' Katie Evans is head of research and policy at Money and Mental Health, a leading charity committed to breaking the link between financial difficulty and mental health problems. 'There are lots of places that can help. Step-Change is one, the Citizens Advice Bureau is another.'

The average person in the UK owes £8k, and that doesn't include their mortgage. A friend recently asked me, 'Are other women like me in debt?', and I could answer her honestly, 'Yes they are.' She believed that she was the only one 'fucking up', as she put it, and because of the shame that surrounds debt I was the first person she had ever told how much debt she was in. With £8k on her credit card she was bang on the UK average.

Considering just how common and how easy it is to fall into debt, those who do are often punished heavily. There is a stigma surrounding debt – it's thought to be the result of spending frivolously or being stupid or selfish with money. 'If you look at media portrayals, reckless spending is often shown to be the cause of debt. If you read the comment sections of the right-wing press, it's judgemental.' Sorana is a spokesperson for StepChange, the leading UK debt charity. It offers free debt advice to anyone, and in the twenty-five years since StepChange was founded, they've helped over 5 million people and repaid £4bn of their debts.

'It's presumed such a situation is squarely the responsibility of the individual,' Sorana continues, 'that it isn't the result of structural inequalities and structural problems with the economy and the labour market. Yet a lot of people are in debt simply to make ends meet.' In 2017, 9.3 million people used credit to meet a household need – such as their gas or electricity bill – with a worrying 1.4 million of this group resorting to 'high-cost' credit, such as payday loans. 'Even if you knew how to manage your money better than Martin Lewis [founder of MoneySavingExpert.com], if your wages don't cover your rent and your bills, you will be getting into debt, regardless of your money skills,' says Sorana. People are expected to be able to keep themselves afloat no matter what life throws at them. Our ability to earn is so intrinsically linked to our self worth that, as Sorana puts it, 'If you are in debt, it can be perceived that you're failing to be a human.'

Considering how much society stigmatises debt, credit and loan companies make it sound very enticing. Every time I log on to my Barclays app there is a small message advertising a loan. I receive credit card offers through the post weekly, once receiving an actual credit card I hadn't applied for, with a 'Just activate and go' sticker on the front of it. Without asking if I wanted it, my credit card company increased the limit on my card to £11,500. That is an amount I would find catastrophic to pay back should I ever spend it.

By the time we're 21, many of us will already be in many thousand pounds' worth of debt. According to the Institute for Fiscal Studies, a student graduating in England in 2018 will leave university in an average of £50,800 debt. Even more worryingly, as students from disadvantaged backgrounds can borrow more in maintenance support (which are now loans rather than grants), the poorest students will graduate with the highest debts. Student loans can be your first experience of debt, and they feel so normal, like everyone is getting one. As Sorana points out, 'Student loans have changed attitudes towards debt in general. It's almost a given now, you expect to be in debt as a young adult.'

I spoke to Bola Sokunbi, the founder of Clever Girl Finance, a cool financial platform whose mission is to increase financial literacy in women. She pointed out the flaws in how we talk about credit, especially to young people: 'Unfortunately we live in a society where debt is called credit. It's marketed as this amazing thing. I see young people fall into that trap – they're all, "I can get money to buy my books, I can get money to pay my rent." I always say, "Don't borrow as much as you can borrow. At the end of the day it's not free money. Get educated on the implications of taking on that debt."'

And it's not just student loans affecting young people. Ironically, people often get into debt when they first start earning money because they overestimate how far their pay packet will stretch – they'll buy a car on finance and then find out that actually £350 a month is more than they can cover comfortably, so they take a credit card out to cover living expenses, and their debt cycle begins.

Sorana tells me that 'while getting into debt is something that could affect absolutely anyone at any point, obviously problem debt affects lower-income families more because they don't have access to any extra money to get them out of trouble and cover a financial need if they fall ill, are made redundant, their hours are reduced at work, or they fall pregnant, whereas people on higher incomes might have that safety net.'

Indeed, a 2017 Aviva report showed that low-income families had on average just £95 of savings and investments, excluding pensions, down from £136 the previous year. Whereas high-income families' savings are increasing year-on-year, averaging at £62,885 up from £50,208 the previous year.

If you don't have savings and you're living pay cheque to pay cheque, and then something happens such as your fridge breaking, using credit to buy a new one probably feels like the easiest solution. Brighthouse is one of the many online retailers that allow you to pay for big-ticket items over many weeks. The less money you have, the more expensive things are. So if a fridge priced at £180.50 is paid for in £3 weekly instalments with a 69.9 per cent interest rate, it means that the eventual amount paid for the fridge will be £468, and it will take over three years to pay off. People get into debt out of necessity, to keep their gas connected or pay for groceries. But vulnerable people are also targeted and enticed to take credit for things they don't need – one in four people who took out a payday loan said they would have gone without the purchase if a payday loan hadn't been available.

The Money Charity estimates that the average person in the UK spends £965 on interest repayments per year. Debt is always the most expensive way to solve any problem, and unfortunately it costs the people with the least amount of money the most. That people are penalised financially for having no money in the first place is a sad fact. Debt is sold as a safety net, but really it's a trap.

'A lot of those we help tell us they've kept their debt secret from friends and family because they were ashamed of the situation that they were in, especially as they were unable to explain how things escalated to such an extent,' Sorana tells me. Claire, a 42-year-old who has cleared £14k of debt (that was spread between a bank loan and credit and store cards), told me the hardest thing was not telling anyone. 'Trying to live life normally and pretend that everything was OK was difficult. I knew I had to sort it, but I didn't want anyone to know the situation. I lost mates. They thought I didn't want to see them, but I was just struggling.' Debt exacerbates many mental health issues. Not only is the pressure of debt stressful, but the shame means people don't seek out the support they need.

Claire isn't alone though. Many of us have struggled with debt at some point, even if it wasn't as big as £14k. Thirty-nine per cent of millennials have gone into debt to keep up with their friends. This is so-called 'FOMO spending'. Seventy-three per cent of those who went into debt to keep up with their friends typically kept it a secret from those friends. Think about that stat: 39 per cent – that's almost two out of every five people, nearly half of a 'friendship group'. I can't help but think that if we were more honest with each other, many friendship groups would happily dial down the spending. Chances are it's not just you going into your overdraft. If you all cut your FOMO spending together there would be nothing to feel FOMO about.

What happens when friends or family become the bank? Because it's not just banks and loan companies who lend money. Sometimes people turn to friends and family to avoid steep interest rates. But borrowing money (even a small loan) off someone close to you can complicate your relationship, as Dan, a 22-year-old, found out. 'I [borrowed] £300 off my older brother for a flight. We'd agreed I'd pay him back in a couple of months when I was due to be paid for a contract. During the time that I owed him money it was awkward to see him. I felt guilty spending in front of him, even buying us both a pint.' And then there's a bigger difficulty – what if you find you can't pay back the money? StepChange advises that 'it can be difficult to talk to someone about this. In many cases you can help resolve the situation by talking through things with your friend or family member and coming to an agreement on how you'll deal with the debt.' Maybe Dan should just say to his brother, 'I'll get us a drink, and don't worry I'm all good to pay you back for that flight next month. Thanks again.' A quick verbal check-in rather than letting the loan be the elephant in the room.

Most people in problem debt wait about eighteen months before they seek debt advice. 'It's ridiculous, because the UK have one of the best free debt advice sectors in the world, and that advice is really really effective,' Katie from Money and Mental Health tells me. 'Most of the time debt problems can be resolved really simply, but people don't seek advice. They allow the debt to pile up with fees and charges on top, and the situation can sadly become more serious.'

No one needs to struggle with debt on their own. Step-Change is just one of the charities and organisations set up to specifically help people with their debt. Citizens Advice is always available too, and then there's Debtors Anonymous – like Alcoholics Anonymous but for 'recovered debtors'. It's a twelve-step programme that relies on a community of people who have struggled with debt helping each other out. Their motto is 'Personal recovery depends upon unity'. They bring people together who understand each other's experience, even providing ongoing support to help keep spending in check once people have paid off their debt.

Debt can be a lonely, isolating experience. We need to share our debt stories, we need to curb our judgement around debt and we need to help each other take back control of our finances and our lives, and that might mean talking to friends, family and partners. As Bola from Clever Girl Finance advises clients who come to her in a money mess, 'Take a deep breath. Forgive yourself for your money mistakes. And get educated. When your finances are in a mess you become overwhelmed and when you're overwhelmed you can get stuck in that self-judgement cycle. Everyone in the world, even the Beyoncés, have made money mistakes, so forgive yourself. Now that you know your mistakes, make sure you ask yourself: what are the lessons? What do I never want to happen again?'

How to get out of debt

Do not ignore debt

The worst thing you can do is ignore your debt. It will not go away if you don't do anything about it, and it will keep spiralling. Speak to someone and make a plan.

No debt problem is unsolvable, and there are steps you can take to get yourself back on steady ground.

Speak to an expert, for free

If you're feeling overwhelmed get in touch with StepChange, or check out one of their online debt plan tools. They are one of many debt charities in the UK who will help you for free. They will help you create a budget and recommend debt solutions that suit your situation. They can even help you apply for any debt solutions they think are right for you, and make sure all the correct paperwork is in place.

Not all debt is bad debt

Debt can generally be sorted into three categories: good debt, bad debt and ugly debt. Work out what debt you have and put it in order of what debt is costing you the most:

Good debt is an investment that will grow, such as a mortgage on a property that is appreciating in value. Good debt can also be necessary debt, like a student loan, or a car loan to be able to get to work.

Bad debt is low-interest debt. Some credit cards and your overdraft fall into this category.

Ugly debt is the worst. This is debt incurred to buy items that quickly lose their value and are most likely worthless before the loan is paid off, and loans whose interest rates are so high they can cause a spiral of having to take loans to pay off loans – such as payday cash advances and doorstep loans.

Understand compound interest

When interviewing financial advisor Simon Russell, I asked him, 'What is the one thing you would like people to know and understand about money?' He answered immediately with two words: 'compound interest'.

Compound interest describes the process of charging – or earning – interest on interest. So if you owe £100 with 10 per cent annual interest and pay it back in year 1, you'll pay £110. If you default until year 2, you'll pay £110 + (10 per cent of 110) = £121. If you default for another year you will pay £121 + (10 per cent of 121) = £133.10. This is why unpaid debt gets bigger and bigger, 'spiralling' into the unmanageable. A vicious cycle ensues that is almost impossible to get out of without help.

Make a plan

- List all of your debts in order of their interest rate.
- Paying off the one with the highest interest rate first makes the most financial sense, although some people find that paying off the smallest debt as quickly as possible gives them a much-needed emotional win.
- Do a budget and work out the maximum amount you can dedicate to debt each month, then work out how to split this across the debts you owe, taking into account that you need to cover minimum monthly payments on every debt you have.
- Get in touch with everyone you owe money to and make a plan with each of them to repay any debts. That way you won't be getting random red letters and court orders. Utility providers, payday loans, store cards and credit cards will all help you create a plan to pay what you can afford, so tell them if you are finding your minimum payments difficult. Some might even be able to freeze the interest.

- Consolidating your debt into a single loan can make it feel more manageable than having lots of loans to keep on top of, but seek advice from somewhere like StepChange first. Some consolidation loans can have even higher interest rates than you're paying.

Get the lowest rates

Can you lower any of your debts' interest rates? First check by calling the creditor and asking. If they won't lower the interest then see if you can transfer to an interest-free credit card. Then follow the golden rule of paying the debt off before the interest-free period ends.

Automate

Set up a direct debit, preferably so you don't see the money in your account before it goes out to pay off your debt.

Go big

Make the maximum payments you can possibly afford. The debt will cost you less in the long run.

Talk to someone close to you

The emotional burden of debt can be debilitating. Again – talk to a friend, tell your family. Even if they are judgemental, I bet the reality of their judgement is less than the judgement you heap on yourself. If you can't find the support you need from the people you know, then groups like Debtors Anonymous get people who are suffering from the same problem together to support each other.

Chill

Once you've created a plan you can stick to there is no point going over past mistakes or constantly stressing. If you stick to the plan, your debt will reduce and eventually you can ...

Get excited

A friend told me about how she got out of debt, and she used words I'd never heard in conjunction with debt: 'I finally realised that no one was going to solve this problem for me. Get excited about it. That's what you should tell your readers. That's how I got out of debt: I envisioned being debt-free and how that would feel, and I genuinely felt excited about the future. Every month I looked forward to making the next payment.'

Celebrate

Getting out of debt can be one of life's great moments. It's a real achievement, and might take more work than college or learning how to drive, so when you get there, make sure you celebrate.

Remember, it's all solvable, and lots of people want to help:

StepChange – 0800 138 1111
Citizens Advice Bureau – www.citizensadvice.org.uk
Samaritans – 116 123

28

Why we mustn't ignore money and mental health

'People who have mental health problems – which is one in four at any given time in the UK – are three times as likely to be in problem debt. And of those with problem debt, half will have a mental health problem,' says Katie Evans (who we heard from in the last chapter), head of research and policy at Money and Mental Health (M&MH). Separately they're two of the hardest things to talk about. Yet they're spooning bedmates, undeniably linked, and they trigger each other rather savagely: mental health issues can cause financial diffi-culty, and financial difficulty can trigger mental health issues. It's the chicken and egg conundrum that many patients find themselves in – which came first, their mental health issues or their money problems?

If we imagine mental health issues on a spectrum of severity, then money causes problems at every single juncture. From lowering our mood, causing mild depression and low-level anxiety to bipolar spending sprees and critical depression in brain-damaged patients. It's paramount that we talk about both of them at the same time, yet the stigma associated with both mental well-being and with financial difficulty means they are both tiptoed around, stigmatised and ignored, allowing the problems created by their convergence to compound even more.

M&MH is an independent charity set up by Martin Lewis to conduct research and help change policy affecting those with money problems and mental health issues. Part of their work is educating regulators, banks, building societies, retailers and energy companies on how to break the link between mental health and money problems. Based on the stats alone, chances are that if a creditor is trying to recover a debt that is in arrears, they will be communicating with someone who has mental health issues, yet M&MH found that people weren't being dealt with in a humane way. 'There are people in crisis care, which means they are in hospital or under the care of a crisis team, and they're there because their life is at risk,' says Evans. 'And we found that people in those situations were getting visits from bailiffs and were being served with eviction notices or court orders for unpaid council tax. It is Dickensian; that just shouldn't be happening.'

It's not just inpatients and people suffering from bipolar who are at risk of getting into problem debt. Many conditions, even those not diagnosed, like mild anxiety, can exacerbate money problems. 'I was diagnosed with general anxiety disorder when I was 22, and I'm pretty good at dealing with the physical and mental ramifications of it now. But my relationship with it and money is something that I didn't even realise I was battling with until very recently.' Maxine, 27, is a freelance actor and part-time administrative assistant. 'I went through a really, really horrible phase of just not checking my bank balance out of complete fear and anxiety, and I hated it.

It was like a self-perpetuated circle of shame. Like, if I check it, I'll see the monetary value of how much shit I've spent this month and then I'll get into a shame spiral.' Maxine's anxiety feeds her bad money habits, which in turn cause further anxiety. 'Spending money is a thousand per cent a ramification of feeling anxious. Which is why, ironically, I'm expecting a couple of packages today.' Mental health issues aren't 'an excuse' for bad money management; it's well recognised in the medical world that mental health problems affect our ability to control impulses, with impulse spending being a clinical symptom across lots of conditions.

Being alone triggers Maxine's anxiety, so she tries to socialise as much as possible, but that in itself causes problems, because socialising costs money she doesn't have. 'It's a weird thing to talk about. I don't know if friends understand. If you say, "I'm not drinking because of this issue" it's like "OK, cool". But if you say "I'm not spending because I have an issue with overspending" – well, I don't think they'd know what to say.'

Someone else finding it difficult to communicate with her friends about money because of her mental health is Georgia, a 22-year-old economics graduate. She struggles with undiagnosed anxiety, and has a particular issue of being assertive when asking for owed money from flatmates. She has been attending workshops with iCope, an NHS service that deals with different facets of anxiety and depression. You can get one-on-one advice over the phone or attend workshops of roughly twenty people. Her flatmates constantly pay their rent late, and this is a huge source of tension for her, and triggers anxiety. Currently Georgia can't ask her flatmates for the money face to face. 'I'm scared about the way I'll say it, because the frustration will have built up. I'm scared that it'll come across quite blunt, or I'll get exasperated.' It's evident when speaking to Georgia that this causes her much anxiety, both the late payments and the difference between her attitude and the attitudes of her flatmates. And, disappointingly, the major roadblock to solving the situation is anxiety around discussing both money and mental health.

Many of us, even if we haven't been diagnosed with a mental health issue, find that the money we have – or rather don't have – determines our moods. Richard Godwin, the journalist who outed his salary in the *Guardian*, talked to me about the mood-altering power of money. 'There have been times when the money hasn't come in. For example, I check my bank account every morning to see what has come in and what has randomly gone out, and if you're down to £50 or something, then it does ruin your mood, the shop windows seem insulting, it can be really damaging to your self. And it poisons relationships because a friend will ask you for lunch and you can't go. So there is a definite correlation with no money and misery, but not a correlation with more money and happy.'

If money affects those of us without mental health issues, imagine what the ups and downs of a bank balance does to someone who has suffered from depression since childhood, as Paul tells me. 'Money tends to be a trigger of both good and bad feelings, and it is closely tied to how I feel about myself. If I am low on money I feel ashamed and of low value, like "I cannot even control my finances", even if it is through circumstances beyond my control. However, when I have lots of money I feel that all is right, and I feel safe in the knowledge that I am functioning.'

Little or no money can make us feel unsafe, and feeling unsafe is very stressful. We might not think of daily stress as a mental health issue, but it is.

A constant battle faced by those who need treatment for mental health issues is the cost, especially if money issues are causing the need for treatment. 'I actually spoke to one of my managers recently about money worries, but they weren't that supportive.' Surprisingly Olivia works in customer services at a major high street bank. 'They basically said, "Sucks to be you, we can't afford to help you."' Olivia disclosed her mental health issues upfront, but feels she's been penalised for this financially ever since. When Olivia last mentioned to her manager that things were getting on top of her, she was made to see their private healthcare advisor, which meant an excess of £60 on her insurance. 'I don't understand my manager. He knows my source of stress is money issues, and he's making me spend money to talk about money issues. It doesn't make sense.'

Even free can be too expensive when it comes to mental health treatment. Karen Corbett, a therapeutic counsellor who volunteers free therapy for vulnerable, low-income patients, told me, 'I have noticed, particularly in my voluntary role, that a person's financial circumstances really affect their access to assistance, even if the treatment costs nothing – having to take time off work unpaid, needing to pay for childcare, the cost of transport, it can all be too much.' I asked Karen what she saw with her patients in terms of how their mental health affected their money. 'It impacts their capacity to manage their day-to-day life – including finances. Everyday chores can become too overwhelming, even with issues such as anxiety and depression, because just like a physical illness, reduced mental health can affect our capacity to function as we would usually.' On top of not being able to do what is expected of us, mental health can also trigger bad behaviour. 'A person who is struggling with low mood or depression may also feel compelled to spend money to feel better or to cheer themselves up, so this can be dangerous if the cycle is continued and a person gets into debt.'

Spending more money is part of the diagnostic criteria of bipolar, so a doctor will look at a patient's spending for evidence that a person has the condition. 'I've found a pile of brand-new underwear, completely not the kind I would normally buy, still with its tags on, at the bottom of my wardrobe after a manic period.' Judy, 62, has been diagnosed with bipolar. 'When my mood is at one extreme or the other I spend money very erratically, and really feel the repercussions when I stabilise.' In a blog on the Mind charity's website one bipolar sufferer lists 'twenty-three Bibles' as some of the things he bought during a manic period. Katie from M&MH explains more. 'Bipolar disorder is characterised by people essentially being in a delusional state, who are usually having grand visions of the future. Quite often they can be exciting new business plans and things like that, so people go out and spend really large sums of money during a manic period.'

Then there is the struggle of maintaining a job if your mental health dives. Some future-facing organisations understand 'mental health days', when an employee needs to take a moment out for the sake of their health. But when days off stack up, covering living costs can get really hard. 'Because of all the time I had off after the overdose, I'm not allowed to take sick leave now.' Colin, 27, talks of the difficulty of maintaining a job after a very low period. 'I've been taking a few odd days off because of flu and stuff, but they've basically said I can't take any more sick days for the rest of the year. I feel like I'm in a cage or something, like I'm being bullied into coming to work when I'm not well.'

How can we better protect people who get into difficulty while ill? Katie and the M&MH team have just secured commitment from the government for a 'breathing space', a debt respite scheme for those in a mental health crisis. Katie explains its importance: 'People will be offered a six-week period when your creditors won't be allowed to contact you, so there will be no more letters through the post, no more phone calls, no more bailiff visits. It will help give people a period when you can really engage in getting help. I hope it incentivises people to go and get the help they need.'

There are other things too; new financial services like Monzo and Starling have a button on their apps that blocks all gambling services (apart from the Lottery) with a single button.

I ask Katie about the morals of stopping someone from spending on a manic period: 'I believe very deeply in the right to do stupid things if that is what you want to do, but at the same time what you want is to enable people to create environments where they have the greatest chance of flourishing. Sometimes just putting a little bit of friction in-between you and the spending can work, like putting a daily spending limit on your debit card.'

Spending during a manic episode is such a likely symptom of having bipolar that it seems naïve to not put something or someone in place when you're feeling OK that will stop you overspending when you're out of control of your own behaviour.

Talking to Katie I realise how many issues there are to solve, and why we must begin to look at money issues as health issues. We often think of the effect of poverty as physical – poorer health care, junk food, harder working conditions – but the mental strain, the stress, the anxiety, the misery of having few choices, both in the supermarket and where you live, are all debilitating. Then even those who might be seen to have 'enough' are teetering on a stressful precipice of not enough. It's crucial that we integrate the conversation of money into the understanding of mental health. Because no matter how big, or how small, a constant worry about money is a mental health issue.

Epilogue

And breathe ... flow, Zen and not thinking about your bank balance at 3 a.m.

I'm earning less money now than when I started writing this book, yet I'm not nearly as anxious about it. Money doesn't stalk my brain like it used to. I might have spent months talking about it, but ironically I no longer really think about it. It doesn't trigger shame, and any envy I had of richer friends has (mostly) dissipated. It doesn't stall conversations or cause me embarrassment, and it doesn't keep me up at 3 a.m. And that's all because I started talking about it.

Look, it's not all perfect. I still find it hard to remind a friend they owe me money, I recently found myself negotiating my salary via email rather than face to face and I check my bank balance a little too often. But generally, I feel at peace with money.

The aim of this book was to put on paper what we've been too embarrassed or scared to say out loud, because sharing stories helps us learn from one another. When you hear what other people do with their money – the good, the bad and the weird – you get a better idea of what to do with your own. I still have friends for whom talking about money is just too difficult. It was etched into their psyche in childhood that it's rude, and they look at me like I've just invited their dad to a menstruation circle when I share the exact figure of my monthly mortgage. 'Appropriate' is difficult to gauge when you're deliberately going against the status quo. Death, masturbation, menopause, mental illness and poo are some of the topics that we'd rather just not talk about. But not talking about them doesn't mean they don't exist. And aren't inappropriate conversations what friendships are made of?

I don't need someone else to tell me what they earn for me to tell them my salary. I'm not looking for a direct exchange, this isn't tit for tat, I just want people to feel less shame around money, and I'm certain that transparency is key to equality so I'm going to keep talking. Everyday issues emerge that are hard to discuss and examine without talking about money: our addiction to fast fashion, financially abusive relationships, universal basic income, the effect of the Bank of Mum and Dad on the property market. I'm starting conversations so we can at least try to tackle these issues together rather than it being everyone for themselves.

One rule of thumb on talking about money that also applies to the subject of sex: showing off and belittling is never OK, but sharing, inspiring and curiosity are. I hope this book has helped remove some of the shame that surrounds money, but I know a chat in real life with someone you trust will be the real breakthrough.

I feel more in control of my finances than ever before. I know why I'm spending, I know what hangovers do to my budget and why Amazon should be visited with care. I know which of my friends can be relied on to give sensible advice. Also, it's only through conversation that I've developed empathy, both for those with more than me, and those with less. Greater honesty around money means as a friendship group we're all a little more aware of each other's situation and emotions. Just as I wouldn't moan to a friend who recently had a miscarriage about my post-pregnancy belly button, I know which friends might be more sensitive about job worries or debt. The simple act of chatting has taken me from anxiety and shame to control and empathy.

I'm not encouraging you to talk about money because money is all that matters; I'm saying talk about money because by making it unutterable we allow it to become a bigger beast than it needs to be. 'You are not something that can be measured in centimeters, or kilograms, or money, or IQ points, or grades, or likes, or followers, or status. The moment you think you can be measured is the moment you reduce yourself.' The bestselling writer Matt Haig wrote that brilliant sentence, and it's so true: you are not your salary, your last pay rise, your debt or where you can afford to go on holiday. Those numbers aren't so shaming that they must never be known by anyone, and like a woman's age or someone's weight, by protecting the numbers we make them more shameful.

Hiding from money is no longer an option.

I hope you feel ready to make your money work for you. Not necessarily in a pumped kind of way, more with a quiet knowledge that you're doing things for the right reasons, that you are in control, that you get to spend time with the people you love and on the things that are important to you. I hope you know all the things you should do with your money, and importantly all the reasons why you don't do them. I hope you feel like you've got this.

Further reading and resources

The School of Life: How to Find Fulfilling Work
Roman Krznaric

This book is part of a brilliant series edited by Alain de Botton. It explores how we often find ourselves chasing money and status when what we really want is fun and purpose. It works almost like a life coach, asking the reader to answer questions such as 'What is your current work doing to you as a person – to your mind, character and relationships?'

Talking to My Daughter About the Economy **Yanis Varoufakis**

Varoufakis sets out to answer a question from his daughter: 'why so much inequality?' Throughout the book he talks directly to his 14-year-old daughter Xenia and very clearly explains complex subjects such as Apolitical Money and The Birth of Market Societies. It's a very human story of how the current economy came into existence.

Bad With Money *podcast by YouTuber* **Gaby Dunn**

It's fresh, honest and wonderfully chatty. In the first series she explores her own financial identity discussing the actual figures in her bank account and what it's like to go from broke to rich in a matter of months. In the second series she gets more serious but no less entertaining and pokes through the injustices of the American financial system.

Where Should We Begin? *podcast by* **Esther Perel**

It's not about money, instead it's about conversation and relationships. Each episode is a different taped counselling session between a couple and Esther Perel. You can learn a lot about how to have a conversation from listening to Perel help others communicate.

MoneySavingExpert.com **Martin Lewis**

Want to know how to save on household bills or what a first-time buyer's ISA is? Then Money Saving Expert has your back. Imagine every bit of practical advice that I haven't included in this book, well, it will all be listed on this website ... pensions, phone bills, credit cards, debt and consumer issues.

moneyandmentalhealth.org and *mind.org*

If money is affecting your mental health or your mental health is affecting your money management, know that you are not alone. Both of these brilliant organisations have practical advice and emotional support.

Refinery29 Money Diaries

You don't need this recommendation from me: I'm sure if you're reading this book you'll have read the fascinating weekly money diaries of various anonymous millennials worldwide.

You Need a Budget (YNAB)

At its heart it's a methodical budgeting app, but its methodology, website videos and podcast provide very helpful money strategies and simple instructions to follow.

Acknowledgements

This book is lucky enough to have been built by some amazing women. It wouldn't have ever happened without Niki Chang first asking, 'Hey, do you think you might want to write a book about money?' Even though she can't remember that conversation, it was the catalyst. She has since transcended agent and become a friend. Her words have scooped me up too many times to count over the past few months. I hope she writes a book too one day because she has so much to say that matters.

If you're going to write about a taboo subject you better have a great editor. Thankfully I had Louisa Dunnigan. She pushed the words when they needed to be pushed and pulled them right back when they weren't working. I was constantly amazed by her tact, composure and passion.

I met Simonne Gnessen when I went to have a session of financial therapy with her for an article I was writing for *ELLE*. She was so calm and reassuring that I was immediately jealous of her actual friends. Simonne was the first person to make me think about money differently and the first to introduce me to the idea of financial therapy. She was so giving of her time for this book – thank you.

Thank you to the other financial therapists I was lucky enough to talk to and quote – Eric Dammann, Brad Klontz, Thomas Faupl and Jennifer Dunkle. Without your brains it would be a very different book.

Thank you to Richard Godwin, Melissa Arnold, Karen Corbett, Matt Hutchinson, Zoe Cohen, Dr Adi Jaffe, Wendy Patrick, David Burkus, Hailley from Buffer, Helen Russell, Pip Jamieson, Caroline Pay, Michelle Kennedy, Lydia Pang, Katriona Fraser, Dr Martino Picardo, Lucy Sheridan, Harriet Allner, Liv Siddall, Brittany Bathgate, Lotte Jeffs, Naomi Oluleye, Missy Flynn, Thomas Davies, Mike Higgins, Bella Webb and Julia Kingsman of The Good Literary Agency. Thank you to Matthew Bolton and Donald Hirsch, both for speaking to me and for the work they do in the campaign for the Living Wage.

Thank you to Anne Boden of Starling Bank and Tom Blomfield of Monzo Bank.

Thank you to financial advisors Royston Fox and Simon Russell for not laughing out loud at the dismal disarray of my finances and for helping to shape them into something I'm proud of. And for making me pay into a pension!

Thank you to Katie Evans from Money and Mental Health, Sorana from StepChange and Bola Sokunbi the founder of Clever Girl Finance.

Thank you to Hannah Nathanson and Lena De Casparis of *ELLE* and Gillian Orr of Refinery29. Without your commissions there wouldn't be a book.

Thank you to Anomaly.

Thank you to Tania Keeling and Marianne Craig.

Thank you to team Serpent's Tail, especially Anna-Marie, Patrick and Flora.

Thank you to my friends and family who had to listen to me talk about money a lot, as well as be subjected to some awkward questioning. Thank you so much for your words which literally fill this book – Bella, Greg, Keren, Abi, Auro, Louisa, Rupert, Laura, Thom, Liam, Sara, Fritha, Mads, Bex, James, Moss, Maisie, Jay, Chris, Ed, Tim, Stuart, Oli, Oli, Sarah, Carin, Luke, Kate, Sam, Jess, Jampot, SB, Emma, Vicky (Sid), Christian, Jamie, Elliot, Grandma Holder and Ali & Geoff.

Thank you to my wonderful Mum and Dad, for your love, your work ethic and of course … for the money you've both given and lent to me over the years.

My own mini family – Mark and Cass, seriously I don't know how you put up with me most of the time, but I am so grateful that you do.

And lastly thank you to all the anonymous people who were prepared to have a conversation with a stranger they met on gumtree. These no-holds-barred chats were some of my favourites.